MISSOURI

MISSOURI BY ROAD

NATIONAL FOREST

URBAN AREA

MILES

0 20 40 60 80

St. Louis

Florissant

St. Charles

St. Peters

Washington

Cape Girardeau

Mark Twain National Forest

Sikeston

Wappapello Lake

Park Hills

Mark Twain National Forest

Taum Sauk Mtn. (1,772 ft.)

Black R.

Poplar Bluff

St. Francis R.

Kennett

Mississippi R.

Rolla

Hannibal

Salt R.

Mark Twain Lake

Fulton

Mark Twain National Forest

Current R.

West Plains

Kirksville

N. Fork Salt R.

Macon

Moberly

Columbia

Gasconade R.

Mark Twain National Forest

Chariton R.

Jefferson City

Osage R.

Lake of the Ozarks

Trenton

Sedalia

Missouri R.

Marshall

Pomme de Terre Lake

Bolivar

Branson

Bull Shoals Lake

Springfield

Thompson R.

Kansas City

Independence

Lees Summit

Warrensburg

South Grand R.

Harry S. Truman Reservoir

Stockton Lake

Nevada

Horse R.

Mark Twain National Forest

Table Rock Lake

Grand R.

Smithville Reservoir

St. Joseph

Spring R.

Joplin

Neosho

Platte R.

Missouri R.

Missouri R.

N E S W

61 24 36 54 70 50 55 67 57 55 155 60 63 65 71 35 29 36 44 51

CELEBRATE THE STATES
MISSOURI

Michelle Bennett

BENCHMARK BOOKS

MARSHALL CAVENDISH
NEW YORK

For my dear parents

Benchmark Books
Marshall Cavendish Corporation
99 White Plains Road
Tarrytown, New York 10591-9001

Library of Congress Cataloging-in-Publication Data

Bennett, Michelle.
Missouri / Michelle Bennett.
p.   cm. — (Celebrate the states)
Includes bibliographical references (p.) and index.
Summary: Discusses the geographic features, history, government, people,
and attractions of the state known as the Show Me State.
ISBN 0-7614-1063-5
1. Missouri—Juvenile literature. [1. Missouri.] I. Title. II. Series
F466.3 .B46 2001   977.8—dc21   99-055969

Maps and graphics supplied by Oxford Cartographers, Oxford, England

Photo research by Candlepants Incorporated

Cover photo: Charles Gurche

The photographs in this book are used by permission and through the courtesy of; *Charles Gurche*: 6-7,14, 16, 20, 109, 114. *Corbis*: Buddy Mays, 10-11; Jim Zuckerman, 21; David Muench, 25;Peter Johnson, 28; Bettmann, 50,71, 91, 92, 94, 96, 99, 130 (right& left), 131, 132, 135 (right&left); Richard Cummins, 56, 106, 107, 111, 118, 138; George Hall, 60; Joseph Sohm, Chromosohm Inc., 61, 68-69; Ted Speigel, 62, 75,83 (left&right), ; Tony Arruza, 64; Tony Hamblin/Frank Lane Picture Agency, 65; Kelly-Mooney, 74 (top); Reuters Newsmedia, 78; Dave G. Hower, 81, 117; Ted Streshinsky, 86; Underwood &Underwood, 101; Julie Habel, 102-103; George Lepp, 121 (left); Derek A. Robinson/Frank Lane Picture Agency, 121 (right); Layne Kennedy, 124 (right); Mike King, 137; Corbis, 134. *Photo Researchers Inc.*: Garry D. McMichael, 13; M.H. Sharp, 23 (top); Suzanne L. Collins & Joseph T. Collins, 23 (lower); Gary Retherford, 26; Mslowski Photos, 124 (left). Albert A. Kost (American, b. St. Joseph, Missouri), *Missouri Woods In Winter* watercolor 1983.464, Collection of the Albrecht-Kemper Museum of Art, St. Joseph Missouri: 30-31. National Museum of American Art, Washington DC, Art Resourse, NY: 33. Missouri Historical Society: 34, 35 (both), 40, 41, 45, 48, 49, 95. The Saint Louis Art Museum, 37. Randall Hyman: 52-53, 66, 74-75, 88-89, 105, 127, 128, back cover. Laura Ingalls-Wilder Association, Mansfield, MO: 97.

Printed in Italy

5   6   4

CONTENTS

MISSOURI IS . . .

Missouri is right at the center of America.

"A Missourian gets used to Southerners thinking him a Yankee, a Northerner considering him a cracker, a Westerner sneering at his effete Easternness, and the Easterner taking him for a cowhand."
—William Least Heat–Moon, Missouri writer

Missourians come from rugged stock . . .

"They were a rough, uneducated class, delighting in fighting and quarreling, but in the main hospitable."
—Joseph McGee, a settler in northwestern Missouri, 1837

"Missourians take pride in not obeying the laws."
—David Goodman, St. Louis native

. . . and they are still resourceful and self-reliant.

"It's a do-it-yourself culture." —David Goodman, St. Louis native

Missourians are a bit old-fashioned . . .

"Missouri, though some Missourians may not like to hear it, is a rural-minded country. The flavor of a premachine-age past hangs in its drawling speech. In the skepticism of its people there is a good deal of the old doubting backwoods farmer who isn't going to be dragged into newfangled situations without long consideration. Missouri is a state which does not rush wildly to decision."
—painter Thomas Hart Benton

. . . a bit skeptical . . .

"I am from Missouri: you have got to show me."

—Missouri congressman Willard Vandiver

. . . and sometimes leery of strangers.

"Not much traffic comes through some of those places. If an outsider comes over the hill, wearing something different or doing something curious, they are not hesitant to look you straight in the face and check you out." —Matt Statler, Jackson, Missouri native

And they like to tell a tall tale now and then.

"Missouri grows the biggest liars in the world."

—Vance Randolph, collector of Ozark folklore

Missouri is sometimes called the Show Me State. Its citizens have a stubborn skepticism and self-reliance that have served them well through the centuries. Even today, the wildness of Missouri's early years remains rooted in its citizens' souls, and they would rather not be ruled by many laws.

Missouri is a mixture of many things: bustling cities and peaceful meadows, factories and rugged hills. Let's explore the state that gave the world ragtime music, Kansas City barbecue sauce, and Huckleberry Finn. Let's explore Missouri.

1 IN THE HEART OF THE HEARTLAND

The Missouri landscape is like a crazy quilt with three basic patterns. Rolling grassland covers its northern third and a wedge along the west; in the south are rocky, forested hills; and in the southeast lie flat, swampy lowlands.

GRASSLANDS AND BLUFFS

Northern Missouri is rolling farmland, largely blanketed with green and golden crops like corn, soybeans, and wheat. Its grassy slopes also feed herds of grazing cattle.

The Missouri River writhes across the middle of the state from west to east, where it pours into the Mississippi River at the state's eastern edge. The source of the Missouri River is in Montana, where it runs clear and clean. By the time it has traveled to Missouri—more than two thousand miles—it has picked up enough dirt to earn its nickname, the Big Muddy.

South of the Missouri River, the land grows more hilly. The hills become yellowish white limestone bluffs, topped with oak trees and covered with short reddish grass that looks like fox fur. In some places, the grasses explode into bloom. Missourian Paulette Hale describes Lead Mine Conservation Area, near Springfield, as "a wildflower paradise. Purple coneflower, pale yellow louse wort, . . .

The low, grassy hills of northern Missouri make ideal cattle-grazing land.

fire red cardinal flower and various shades of violets splash the hillsides with color."

THE RUGGED OZARK HILLS

South-central Missouri is a rocky land full of streams, lakes, woods, and caves. This is the Ozark Plateau, an ancient highland of craggy ridges and narrow ravines. This area is home to the state's highest point, Taum Sauk Mountain. It stands 1,772 feet above sea level—which is not very high. But the roads over the Ozark hills are steep and winding. "If you get carsick it's a terrible place to be," says Matt Statler, recalling family trips through the region.

The "downcutting" of rivers in the Ozarks has produced deep river canyons. Downcutting occurs when a river flows across soft rock, such as limestone. The river's water, sand, and stones carve deeper and deeper into the rock, resulting in steep cliffs and rivers that rush at the bottoms of rocky gorges. Dramatic downcutting

Johnson's Shut-Ins State Park near Piedmont is full of handsome river canyons carved by rushing water.

can be found at Johnson's Shut-Ins State Park, named for the narrow canyons that enclose its rivers. The rock has been smoothly scooped out by the flowing water. You can slither down these natural water slides, with or without an inner tube. The "shut-ins" are a favorite destination on hot summer days. "It's full of crazy rock formations," says John Meyer, who grew up nearby. "And there's a little cliff you can jump off of, into the water."

In the northern Ozarks, near the center of the state, is the Lake of the Ozarks region. Lake of the Ozarks is a sprawling, many-tentacled lake made by damming the Osage River. Visitors flock to this region to enjoy boating and fishing in a gorgeous setting.

MISSISSIPPI RIVER BOTTOMLANDS

As you head east from the Ozarks, the land slopes down to the winding Mississippi River, which forms Missouri's eastern border. In some places, the shore is a flat expanse of dark, grayish mud. In others, swamps filled with plants such as foxtail and nut grass provide shelter and food for many creatures, including migrating birds. Southeast Missourian Louise Brown looks forward to goose flight season, because she and her husband "can watch the snow geese and Canada honkers by the thousands. . . . For retired farmers like us, it's great entertainment at no cost."

LIVING WITH FLOODS

Missouri's rivers usually flood in the spring, when melting snow from the Rocky Mountains flows into tributaries of the state's two

At Otter Slough Conservation Area, visitors can enjoy the beauty of southeastern Missouri's swampland. Some rare species of fish, like the pugnose minnow, live here.

HAZARDS OF THE MISSISSIPPI

The Mississippi River is full of hidden dangers for boats. Large, submerged tree branches, called snags, can catch boats and tear a hole in them or tip them over. Boats sometimes run aground on shoals, places where sand and mud have piled up so that they almost touch the surface of the water.

Another type of rough spot occurs where one river flows into another. For instance, the Missouri River pours into the Mississippi River eighteen miles north of downtown St. Louis. The Big Muddy hits with such force that it crosses the powerful Mississippi River and actually carves a deep notch into the opposite bank before swirling downstream and mixing with the "Father of Waters."

Father Jacques Marquette, a French missionary who traveled down the Mississippi River in a birchbark canoe in 1673, wrote of this spot: "We were rowing peacefully in clear, calm water when we heard the noise of a rapids into which we were about to fall. I have seen nothing more dreadful. An accumulation of large and entire trees, branches and floating islands was issuing forth from the mouth of the [Missouri] river, . . . we could not without great danger risk passing through it."

largest rivers, the Missouri and Mississippi. Heavy spring rains also swell the rivers. Water sometimes covers farms, drowning chickens, pigs, and cows. Homes can be washed away. Sometimes whole towns are swamped.

Devastating floods struck Missouri in 1993. The Missouri River got so high that the people of Rhineland decided to move the whole town. While 157 of the town's residents decided to rebuild their houses on higher ground, one chose to stay in old Rhineland.

LAND AND WATER

Map legend:
- 1,500 – 3,000 ft.
- 600 – 1,500 ft.
- 300 – 600 ft.
- 0 – 300 ft.

MILES
0 20 40 60 80

Cities and features:
St. Louis
Florissant
St. Charles
St. Peters
Washington
Cape Girardeau
Sikeston
Kennett
Park Hills
Poplar Bluff
Rolla
West Plains
Fulton
Hannibal
Kirksville
Macon
Moberly
Columbia
Jefferson City
Sedalia
Trenton
Marshall
Independence
Lees Summit
Warrensburg
Kansas City
Nevada
Bolivar
Springfield
Joplin
Neosho
Branson
St. Joseph

Rivers and water features:
Mississippi R.
Missouri R.
Meramec R.
Black R.
St. Francis R.
Wappapello Lake
Taum Sauk Mtn. ▲ (1,772 ft.)
Current R.
Gasconade R.
Salt R.
Mark Twain Lake
N. Fork Salt R.
Charriton R.
Osage R.
Terre Lake
Lake of the Ozarks
Harry S. Truman Reservoir
South Grand R.
Thompson R.
Grand R.
Platte R.
Smithville Reservoir
Pomme de Terre R.
Stockton Lake
Niangua R.
Spring R.
Table Rock Lake
Bull Shoals Lake
Missouri R.

Compass:
N
W   E
S

Eighty-four-year old Ransom Doll had lived there almost fifty years and didn't plan on leaving. "My house is built up high," he later explained. "The river only got in my house once in 500 years, back in '93, and 500 years from now, I don't care how high it gets."

THROUGH THE SEASONS

Missouri offers a pretty complete selection of weathers. Winters can be harsh, but are more often mild. Missouri's snowfalls average fifteen inches per year, but even after a heavy snowfall, the snow usually lasts less than a week. And summers, says one St. Louis native, are "hot and humid. . . . The concrete sidewalks stay hot almost until midnight."

Fall can bring rain, alternating with cool, sunny, perfect autumn weather. Spring is downright beautiful in Missouri, especially in the Ozarks, where the white-flowered dogwood trees bloom in the fresh woodland air. According to one legend, Missourians in heaven must be tied up. "If they were not chained," relates Missouri historian Carl W. Smith, "they would all return to the Ozarks in the spring."

MIXED AIRS

Above Missouri, masses of air from other parts of the country come together like a big square dance in the sky. Warm, damp air travels up from the Gulf of Mexico. Air from the southwest is dry and hot. And from the north comes cold Canadian air. When these different air masses crash together it can cause sudden, sometimes violent, changes in weather.

Missouri's Ozark forests abound with dogwood trees, which usually bloom around May 1. "They are a celebration of confetti across a reawakening landscape," exults writer Diane Calabrese.

About the most violent form of weather in Missouri is the tornado, or twister. When a strong updraft of wind hits a whirl of rotating air, a tornado is formed. The funnel-shaped wind moves along the ground at speeds of up to three hundred miles per hour, tearing up everything in its path. The worst tornado ever recorded in the United States passed through Missouri, Illinois, and Indiana on March 18, 1925, killing 695 people and causing millions of dollars worth of damage. Missouri averages twenty-seven tornadoes a year.

Tornadoes can cause spectacular damage. After a tornado hit the building where he works, Steve Okenfuss of Kansas City remarked, "It looks like a big foot just smashed it."

Sometimes straight wind storms can wreak as much havoc as a twister. After a severe storm, "you'll see some toy you had in your garage in somebody else's yard, a mile away," mused one Missouri native. "I saw my sister's umbrella down by the school, a month later."

The variable climate of Missouri is even more variable in the Ozarks, where it can be foggy in one valley and sunny in the next one, just a few miles away. One old Ozark man said of weather predictions, "Them government weathermen do pretty well on a flat prairie, like Kansas or western Oklahoma, but they ain't worth a damn in a hilly country."

PLANTS AND ANIMALS

Missouri is rich in plant and animal life. The Ozarks' steep hills and narrow valleys are home to oak and hickory trees, skunk cabbages, bluebells, jack-in-the-pulpits, and wild hyacinths. White-tailed deer, red and gray squirrels, and wild turkeys frequent these forests, feeding on acorns and hickory nuts. Raccoons, opossums, and skunks roam about at night. The rocky Ozark hills are legendary for their poisonous but shy copperhead snakes.

Woodchucks and cottontail rabbits graze in the borders between woods and meadows. In upland meadows, wildflowers like bright red Indian paintbrush thrive in the thin, rocky soil.

The low, rolling meadows in the north-central part of the state are sprinkled with cedar and hardwood trees and teeming with birds. Red-tailed hawks coast the sky, watching for white-footed mice on the ground. The prairie is covered with tall grasses and

The curious, ring-tailed raccoon eats just about anything, but lives mainly on insects, mice, and fish.

The copperhead's pattern of brown blotches helps it blend in with the ground. Here, a baby snake blends in with its mother, except for the bright yellow tip of its tail.

THE NEW MADRID EARTHQUAKE

Normally when people think of earthquakes in the United States, they think of California. But the second-largest earthquake in U.S. history occurred in the middle of the country, in southeastern Missouri! At 2 A.M. on December 16, 1811, an earthquake hit the small river town of New Madrid, jolting sleepers from their beds. People fled from their homes, believing the end of the world had come. Rumbling filled the darkness; houses crashed to their foundations. The earth cracked open, spewing sand and chunks of blackened wood.

On the Mississippi River, enormous waves swallowed up islands, and the riverbanks fell in, carrying large trees with them. By the next day, the river had changed course and the town was fifteen feet lower than before. The earthquake was equivalent to 8 or higher on the Richter scale, and its shocks were felt as far away as New York City.

The New Madrid Fault, which caused the 1811 quake, underlies a long stretch of the Mississippi River. In fact, minor earthquakes rattle through the area quite frequently, but many are too small even to be felt. Others are noticeable but do not do much damage. One quake, in May 1991, measuring 4.6 on the Richter scale, was felt in six states. But it was not serious. "It was a 'dish' tremor," said Robert Latham, a sheriff's dispatcher. "It just shook the dishes."

wildflowers where millions of bison once grazed. Some species of grasses grow ten feet tall, waving in the wind like a strange sea. The prairies are sometimes swathed with white ox-eye daisies and bright orange butterfly weed.

Missouri's rivers, streams, and wetlands abound with fish, turtles, frogs, mussels, beavers, waterbirds, and insects. Along the rivers grow trees like sycamore, cottonwood, silver maple, and box elder. Spring flooding washes away the previous year's dead leaves, leaving a layer of fresh mud where tree seeds sprout and grow. Since the river bottom stays so damp, trees thrive even in years with little rainfall. As a result, the bottomlands are often filled with a quickly growing forest of towering trees.

A French explorer, Etienne Veniard de Bourgmont, described the bountiful grasslands around the Missouri River in 1714: "The prairies there are like seas and full of wild beasts, especially buffalo, cows, hinds and stags, which are in numbers that stagger the imagination."

CAVES FOR TOURISTS, CAVES FOR BATS

Missouri has an abundance of natural caves—over 5,500—more than any other state! In many of these caverns grow bizarre rock formations, resembling gigantic icicles, mouthfuls of monstrous teeth, or massive organ pipes. Tourists flock to see these natural wonders. But what's good for tourism isn't necessarily good for the creatures that live in and around the caves.

Bats in particular need caves. Of the thirteen bat species in Missouri, nine live in caves and abandoned mines, hibernating there in the winter. When humans intrude upon their hibernation,

Bats are the only mammals that can fly. When they swoop above people's heads outdoors, they are actually catching insects that swarm above warm human bodies.

the bats fly out of their shelters and die of exposure to the cold. Bats are also left out in the cold when humans seal up their caves and mines. In Missouri, the gray bat and the Indiana bat are in danger of extinction. However, Missouri conservationists and the U.S. government have teamed up to help protect them. They have installed special gates on abandoned mines allowing bats, but not people, to pass in and out.

Many creepy legends surround bats, but in fact bats are quite beneficial to humans. They eat insects and distribute plant seeds with their droppings. One thousand bats can eat more than a ton of insects per year—about 660 million insects—including crop-damaging pests and that warm-weather nuisance, mosquitoes. The little brown bat, another Missouri inhabitant, can consume up to six hundred mosquitoes in an hour.

TURNING WASTEWATER INTO WETLANDS

Eagle Bluffs Conservation Area is a vast expanse of marshy grass-land, with scattered groves of water-loving shrubs at the base of a tall limestone cliff. Who could guess that its clean, fresh water, where ducks dive and deer wade, comes from nearby Columbia's sewage treatment plant?

With their abundant supply of seeds and fish, wetlands make a great rest stop for migrating birds. They also provide a safe place for floodwaters to rise without washing away farms and towns. In 1987, the Missouri Department of Conservation planned to increase the wetlands near Columbia by turning 3,700 acres of farmland back into wetlands. At the same time, Columbia, a fast-growing city, needed to expand its water treatment facility. The citizens of Columbia decided to combine the two projects, building a wastewater treatment facility that would also be an important wildlife refuge and recreation area.

The cleaned, treated wastewater could have been poured directly into the Missouri River, but instead it is strained through a series of special ponds. The ponds are lined with clay and full of living plants, which filter the water again, making it even cleaner than the law requires.

Now, this restored marshland is home to more than 120 species of birds, as well as river-bottom creatures like beaver, raccoon, and fox.

And it's not just for wild creatures to enjoy: a hiking and biking trail connects the conservation area to downtown Columbia. "Everybody came out winners," says Jim Loveless, a biologist at Eagle Bluffs. "The city found a way to dispose of its wastewater, the Department of Conservation got a free water source for an important wetlands project, and after the water is filtered through all these ponds, it actually improves the quality of the Missouri River when it joins it."

By conserving the state's natural resources such as wetlands, wild prairies, and forests, and protecting the creatures that live in them, Missourians can enjoy these treasures for many years to come.

Migratory birds like these Canada geese need to take rest stops during their long trips. They relax in the wetlands along rivers and eat the roots and seeds of water plants.

2 MOTHER OF THE AMERICAN WEST

Missouri Woods in Winter, by Al Kost

Al Kost

Missouri has a turbulent history, and its location is part of the reason: it has literally been "in the middle of things" across the centuries. Its fertile soil has lured settlers since prehistory. Its rivers brought traders, who promoted industry, which provided the goods for even more restless adventurers to pack up and move on. Missouri's natural bounty and human enterprise combined to make it the Mother of the American West.

THE FIRST MISSOURIANS

About A.D. 1000 a great city called Cahokia thrived near present-day St. Louis. The Cahokians hunted deer and bison with stone-tipped arrows, and fished with hooks carved from shells. They also farmed corn, beans, and squash. Traveling in canoes, they were part of a trade network up and down the Mississippi and its connecting rivers. The Cahokians exchanged salt, corn, and stone tools for copper from the Great Lakes and seashells and sharks' teeth from the Gulf of Mexico.

The Cahokians built large earthen mounds. Some of these mounds were impressive graves for important Cahokians. Others were likely used for ceremonies, where Cahokians might worship the sun and birds. The largest of these, Monk's Mound, covers fourteen acres and is one hundred feet tall. It took three hundred years to build, one basketful of dirt at a time.

Over the centuries, the mild climate, fertile land, and abundant wildlife of Missouri's river bottomlands attracted other native peoples. The Missouri, Shawnee, Delaware, Piankashaw, Peoria, Iowa, Sauk, and Fox Indians all lived in Missouri at one time or another. The most prominent Missouri-based tribe was probably the Osage, who lived near present-day Jefferson City. Their villages consisted of cone-shaped huts and larger, oblong buildings made of poles covered with woven grass. Like the Cahokians, the Osage hunted deer, elk, bison, and bear, and planted gardens of corn, beans, and pumpkins.

The Osage were tall, often six feet or more, and were fast runners.

George Catlin's 1834 painting Wa-ho-beck-ee, A Handsome Brave *shows the typical garb of an Osage man.*

The men wore a red or blue loincloth, with deerskin leggings and moccasins, and a blanket carried over one shoulder. The women wore a wrap skirt, leather tunic, and moccasins.

EXPLORERS AND FUR TRADERS

Two of the earliest whites in the Missouri area were Canadian explorer Louis Jolliet and French missionary Jacques Marquette. During their 1673 canoe trip down the Mississippi River, they met the Peoria Indians, who were friendly and generous, sharing with them a meal of corn, fish, and wild ox. About a decade later, in 1682, French explorer René-Robert Cavelier, Sieur de La Salle, stood at the mouth of the Mississippi River and claimed the entire river valley for France.

No government official was sent from France, however. Instead, fur trappers and missionaries scouted the region, made maps of its rivers, and traded with the Indians. The French hoped to profit from the area's beavers, muskrats, and otters. Trappers caught these animals and sold their skins to fur traders. The traders shipped big bales of pelts from trading posts along the rivers, to the eastern United States and Europe. In 1764, French fur traders Pierre Laclede and Auguste Chouteau founded the village of St. Louis at one of these trading posts.

In the late 1700s, Spain took control of the area from France. When France reclaimed it in 1800, the region had more people and more settlements, but otherwise little had changed. French was still the main European language spoken there, and most of the towns' names were French.

The Founding of St. Louis, *by August Becker*

MISSOURI TERRITORY

But France wasn't sure it wanted all that empty land. Explorers and prospectors had found no gold or silver, and Indians living there were not always pleased to see Europeans. Furthermore, France was in the middle of a war with Great Britain, and it simply could not spare the money to keep the colony going.

So, in 1803, France sold the "Louisiana territory" to the U.S. government for $15 million. The Louisiana Purchase encompassed all the land west of the Mississippi that drained into that river. This turned out to be fourteen future states, including Missouri. In

Meriwether Lewis was enthusiastic about his westward expedition with William Clark. One observer said of him, "He will be much more likely, in case of difficulty, to push too far, than to [go back] too soon."

The Lewis and Clark expedition was full of dangerous episodes, from fighting with hostile Indians to running away from bears. When the explorers reached their goal, the Pacific Ocean, on November 7, 1805, it is no wonder that William Clark wrote, "Ocean in view! O! The joy!"

1804, explorers Meriwether Lewis and William Clark set forth from St. Louis to map the Louisiana Purchase and discover a route to the West Coast.

At the time Missouri was a rough and lawless place. Hunters, fishers, and trappers wandered the Ozark forests. Merchants, traders, and craftsmen clustered in trading posts and villages like St. Louis, as did boatmen and laborers.

Missouri's boisterous riverboatmen often tried to outdo each other, not just in fighting and cursing, but also in having a good time. In this George Caleb Bingham painting, a boatman dances a jig as his fellows cheer him on.

The legendary riverboatman Mike Fink came from this stock. Tales of his deeds range from amazing to unbelievable. One of his favorite pastimes was shooting a tin can off a friend's head at forty yards. He never missed. He did once kill a man this way, but Fink claimed that was on purpose. He boasted: "I'm half wild horse and half cock-eyed alligator and the rest o' me is crooked snags an' red-hot snappin' turkle." Many people wished there were fewer types like Mike Fink around. One woman wrote of her Missouri town in 1807: "Cape Girardeau is a very beautiful place but it is very wicked. . . . The main way the men spend their Sundays is in drinking and gambling, horse racing and chicken fighting." One New Englander branded Missouri "a grand reservoir for the scum of the Atlantic states."

Scum or not, newcomers kept coming to Missouri. Some just passed through on their way west, but many stayed for the good farmland, for the abundant hunting, or to be part of the burgeoning cities. Kansas City, once an outpost for pioneers traveling farther west, became a thriving city. It was the center of the state's livestock and grain market.

As white people moved across the land to hunt and settle where the Indians were living, conflicts inevitably arose. Little by little, the U.S. government bought and took land from the Indians, pushing them farther west. The Indians often fought back, but the U.S. Army's superior weaponry—more guns, bullets, and gunpowder— made it a losing battle.

In 1816, about five thousand Indians still lived in Missouri Territory. By 1825 the Osage had surrendered their lands in Missouri and moved to Kansas. By 1838, nearly all of Missouri's

American Indians had been herded out of the state and onto reservations in Kansas and Oklahoma.

THE MISSOURI COMPROMISE AND DRED SCOTT

So many people came to Missouri Territory that by 1818, the population was large enough to petition for statehood. But becoming a state was not simple. At the time, half of the Union's twenty-two states were slave states, and half were free states. Many Missourians owned slaves, and they wanted Missouri to be a slave state. In what was known as the Missouri Compromise, Congress decided to admit Missouri as a slave state, if a free state was admitted at the same time. Thus, in 1821, Missouri was admitted to the Union as the twenty-fourth state. Maine, a free state, had been admitted in 1820 as the twenty-third.

Despite this compromise, tensions over slavery continued to increase across the nation. The 1857 Dred Scott decision pushed these tensions almost to a breaking point. Dred Scott was a slave, owned by a Dr. John Emerson. Together they traveled to, and lived in, free states before returning to Missouri. Emerson died in 1843. After trying unsuccessfully to buy his freedom, Scott filed a suit claiming he should be free because he had lived for four years in free states. The case went all the way to the U.S. Supreme Court. But the Court ruled that Scott must remain a slave. Chief Justice Roger B. Taney, who wrote the decision, asserted that black people were "so far inferior, that they had no rights which the white man was bound to respect." The racism and injustice of this decision made antislavery Northerners even angrier at the proslavery South.

After the controversial Dred Scott decision, the growing tension between slave states and free states caused Abraham Lincoln to proclaim, "a house divided against itself cannot stand. . . . The government cannot endure permanently half slave and half free."

CIVIL WAR

In 1861, the United States went to war—against itself. The Northern states—the Union—were fighting the Southern states—the Confederacy. The underlying issue was slavery.

Compared to other Southern states, Missouri did not have many slaves. Before 1800, several hundred African slaves had been brought to work in Missouri lead mines. Later migrants from Kentucky,

Tennessee, Virginia, and other slave states came to Missouri with their slaves. Even so, by 1860, less than 10 percent of Missourians were slaves. In fact, Missouri contained more Unionists than Confederates. The state provided 40,000 troops to the Confederacy, and 110,000 to the Union.

Being a border state between the North and the South, Missouri was caught in the middle. Large-scale battles between the Union and Confederate armies raged; 1,162 battles were fought in Missouri, the third-highest number of any state. Meanwhile, William C. Quantrill and his gang of proslavery ruffians wreaked havoc, burning houses, looting towns, and killing Union sympathizers. Missouri-born Jesse James rode with Quantrill's raiders.

Although Unionists outnumbered Confederates in Missouri, the Missouri State Guard followed their pro-South governor, Claiborne Jackson, into battle to fight for the Confederate side.

JESSE JAMES

"Between eight and nine o'clock yesterday morning Jesse James, the Missouri outlaw . . . was instantly killed by a boy twenty years old, named Robert Ford. In the light of all moral reasoning, the shooting was unjustifiable; but the law was vindicated, and the $10,000 reward offered by the state for the body of the brigand will doubtless go to the man who had the courage to draw a revolver on the notorious outlaw even when his back was turned, as in this case." (St. Joseph, Missouri, *Evening News*, April 3, 1882)

The Mr. Howard referred to in the song was an alias Jesse James had adopted while in hiding.

It was Robert Ford, that dirty little coward,
I wonder how he does feel.
For he ate of Jesse's bread and he slept in Jesse's bed,
And he laid poor Jesse in his grave. *Chorus*

How the people held their breath when they heard of Jesse's death,
And wondered how he ever came to die.
It was one of the gang, called Little Robert Ford,
That shot poor Jesse on the sly. *Chorus*

Jesse was a man, a friend to the poor,
He would never see a man suffer pain.
And with his brother Frank he robbed the Chicago bank,
And stopped the Glendale train. *Chorus*

It was on a Wednesday night, the moon was shining bright,
They stopped the Glendale train.
And the people they did say, for many miles away,
It was robbed by Frank and Jesse James. *Chorus*

They went to a crossing not very far from there,
And there they did the same.
With the agent on his knees, he delivered up the keys
To the outlaws, Frank and Jesse James. *Chorus*

It was on a Saturday night, Jesse was at home,
Talking to his family brave.
Robert Ford came along like a thief in the night,
And laid poor Jesse in his grave. *Chorus*

This song was made by Billy Gashade,
As soon as the news did arrive.
He said there was no man with the law in his hand,
Who could take Jesse James while alive. *Chorus*

After the war he became a famous outlaw with a gang of his own.

Shortly before the war ended in 1865, slavery in Missouri was abolished. More than 100,000 African-American men, women, and children in Missouri were now free. And homeless. And jobless.

Some African Americans moved to large cities, where they had a chance of finding work in mills and factories, or as maids and servants. Some moved north. Most, lacking the resources to move away, stayed where they were, often living in horrible poverty. Some continued working for the same landowners who had once owned them, for wages little better than slavery. As one former slave put it, they now had "nothing but freedom."

RIVERBOATS AND RAILROADS

The Civil War changed many things. During the war, Missouri's trade to the south stopped, including its river trade.

In 1817, cheering crowds had greeted the *Zebulon Pike* when it became the first steamboat to chug up the Mississippi River from New Orleans to St. Louis. Soon, many steamboats plied the river. At the time, riverboats were the cheapest way to transport heavy goods and faster than traveling over land.

Since it cost money and time to send raw materials to the East to be processed, mills were built along the Mississippi. Flour and lumber mills sprang up in Hannibal and other towns to grind grain from Iowa, and to cut logs from Wisconsin and Minnesota.

Riverboats were not a perfect means of transport, however. They frequently capsized on the treacherous rivers. Collisions, explosions, grounding, and hitting submerged logs and rocks all took

In the mid-1800s, racing steamboats down a stretch of the Mississippi River was a popular pastime. However, train travel gradually made steamboating obsolete, and by 1900, according to reporter Carl Landrum, "half a dozen steamboats at a river landing was a rare sight."

their toll. Accidents wrecked about a third of all steamboats built before 1849.

In 1851, railroad construction began in Missouri. Over the next decade, railroads crisscrossed the state and connected Missouri with the East and West Coasts. Trains were faster than barges or steam-boats, and they could go where the boats could not—over the land. The steamboat, once a symbol of progress and prosperity for towns along the big rivers, became a reminder of a bygone era.

ST. LOUIS AND THE GILDED AGE

In Missouri, all railroads led to St. Louis. In the early nineteenth century, the city had grown from a fur-trading post into a thriving metropolis. By 1850, its mills produced half a million barrels of flour a year. The city also exported bacon, beef, corn, oats, and apples. Some factories made steamboat engines, iron stoves, orna-mental ironwork, and lead pipe. Others brewed beer or turned cotton and wool into cloth. Immigrants from Germany, Ireland, Italy, and Czechoslovakia supplied St. Louis with cheap labor, skilled workers, and businesspeople.

The city profited from the great westward movement of the 1850s. St. Louis outfitted travelers with clothing, food, tools, and machinery. As it continued to "mother" the West, St. Louis itself flourished, building civic and cultural institutions. St. Louis University was established in 1832, and the University of Missouri was founded in 1839—the first state university west of the Mississippi River. During the 1850s, the city instituted a public school system.

By the 1870s, St. Louis had grown into a major manufacturing city with a population of almost half a million. But all this growth had a cost. The noises, smells, and wastes of progress overwhelmed the city. Factories, fueled with coal, spewed black smoke from their chimneys. Factory owners were growing rich, but the people labor-

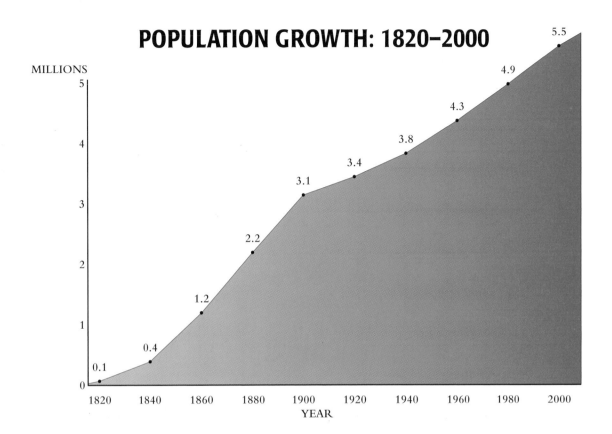

POPULATION GROWTH: 1820–2000

MILLIONS

0.1 • 0.4 • 1.2 • 2.2 • 3.1 • 3.4 • 3.8 • 4.3 • 4.9 • 5.5

YEAR

ing in the factories were paid little and remained abjectly poor, living in crowded slums. "Greater futures enjoyed by a few—hard times suffered by many," was a common lament.

The late nineteenth century was called the Gilded Age, because it was a time when expensive decoration was covering up decay and misery. Missouri author Mark Twain wrote cynically in 1871, "What is the chief end of man?—to get rich. In what way?—dishonestly, if we can; honestly if we must." Many ambitious folks in St. Louis seemed to make this their motto. By the turn of the century, St.

St. Louis was a thriving industrial city in the late nineteenth century. According to writer Theodore Dreiser, "The streets and sky were full of smoke."

Louis had gained a reputation for appalling political corruption, with city officials often accepting bribes from businesses.

THE TWENTIETH CENTURY

Even so, turn-of-the-century St. Louis had a promising future. The 1904 world's fair at St. Louis wowed the entire country with its spectacular exhibits and innovations. Missouri's other big city, Kansas City, was also flourishing, providing the country with hogs, cattle,

THE ST. LOUIS EXPO

Skate on an ice rink through an artificial blizzard—in the middle of summer! Send a telegraph message to a city 1,500 miles away! Gaze upon the first moving pictures you have ever seen, and catch a glimpse of life in exotic, far-off lands: Eskimo igloos, Zuñi cliff dwellings, real live yodelers from the Tyrolean Alps. These things are unremarkable today, but in 1904 they were astonishing. As a fair-goer with the nineteenth century still fresh in your mind, the 1904 world's fair had almost everything you could think of—and many things you couldn't.

The fair celebrated the hundredth anniversary of the Louisiana Purchase and the accomplishments of St. Louis and the Midwest. Elaborately ornamented buildings were constructed and filled with the latest innovations and samples of cultures from around the world. Eye-catching displays showed off the state's best in agriculture, livestock, mining, and fine arts.

It was here that Americans bit into the first hot dogs served in buns, sipped the first iced tea, and tasted the first cotton candy, called "fairy floss." And it was here that an imaginative waffle vendor packed ice cream into a thin waffle, creating the first ice cream cone.

The expo brought St. Louis to the attention of the world. Sometimes it seemed everyone was singing "Meet me in St. Louis, Louis, meet me at the Fair," from a newly popular tune.

wheat, and soybeans. Across the state, universities and public libraries were founded; dams, bridges, and roads were built.

But then, like the rest of America, Missouri sank into the Great Depression of the 1930s. Unemployment skyrocketed as businesses closed. A scorching drought dried up crops and killed livestock. Farm prices fell, wages fell, banks failed, people grew hungry. It was bad all over. The state of Missouri coped with the help of federally funded relief programs. For example, a federal project resettled displaced

After less than twelve weeks as vice president, Truman was thrust into the presidency. Truman confided to reporters, "I don't know whether you fellows ever had a load of hay fall on you, but when they told me yesterday what had happened, I felt like the moon, the stars, and all the planets had fallen on me."

farmers on government farmland, loaning them money for food, live-stock, and seeds.

But things did not really improve until 1941, when the United States entered World War II, and farms and factories geared up for the war effort. In 1945, Missourian Harry S. Truman became vice president. With the death of President Franklin D. Roosevelt three months later he was suddenly faced with the presidency—and the task of ending the war. In August 1945, he ordered the U.S. military to drop two atomic bombs on Japan, demolishing the cities of Hiroshima and Nagasaki and killing 96,000 people. Many more died later from radiation poisoning. But some people believe that even more lives were saved by ending the war quickly.

By this time, manufacturing had replaced agriculture as the state's main employer. Missouri was fast becoming an urban state. By 1970, almost 75 percent of Missourians lived in cities and towns. In the 1980s, Missouri moved into high-technology manu-facturing like the pharmaceutical and aerospace industries. With companies like Monsanto developing genetically engineered crops and computer-electronics factories producing silicon wafers for the nation's computers, Missouri is striding boldly into the twenty-first century.

3 THE GOOD OF THE PEOPLE

The capitol in Jefferson City

All states are united under the U.S. government, but every state also has its own government. Missouri's is based on its constitution, which was first written in 1820. This constitution has been amended several times, when Missourians felt that their basic laws should be changed to adapt to new circumstances. The Missouri state motto is "Let the good of the people be the supreme law."

INSIDE GOVERNMENT

Missouri's state government is divided into three parts: executive, legislative, and judicial.

Executive. The executive branch includes the governor, the lieutenant governor, and other elected and appointed officials. The governor is responsible for making the budget for the state and has the power to sign into law or veto (reject) bills passed by the state legislature. The governor is elected to a four-year term.

Legislative. The legislative branch makes the laws of the state by writing bills and voting on them. The Missouri legislature has a 34-member senate and a 163-member house of representatives. Senators serve a four-year term and house members a two-year term.

Judicial. Missouri's judicial system has three levels. At the lowest level are the circuit courts, commonly known as trial courts. At the next level is the court of appeals, which may review decisions

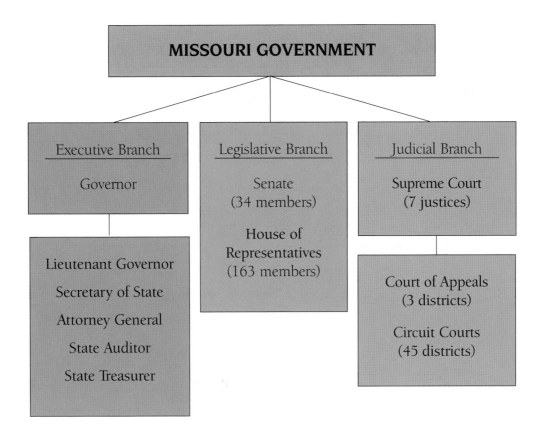

MISSOURI GOVERNMENT

Executive Branch

Governor

Lieutenant Governor

Secretary of State

Attorney General

State Auditor

State Treasurer

Legislative Branch

Senate
(34 members)

House of
Representatives
(163 members)

Judicial Branch

Supreme Court
(7 justices)

Court of Appeals
(3 districts)

Circuit Courts
(45 districts)

made by the circuit courts. At the top is the state supreme court, the final authority on Missouri law. Missouri's supreme court has seven judges, each of whom may serve one twelve-year term, except for the chief justice, who may serve two. The judges are first appointed by the governor from nominations submitted by a judicial selection committee. After judges serve one year, the state's citizens vote on whether they should remain on the court.

THE VOICE OF THE PEOPLE

Missourians have always wanted a say in their government. Two ways they can change the constitution are by initiative and refer-

"I thought working for a casino would be a lot of fun, and it is," says one river-boat casino employee. "But that's if you ignore what you see. I see homeless; I see drunks; . . . [just about every] walk of life comes through these doors."

endum. If enough citizens sign a petition, a proposed change or "initiative" can be put on the ballot, so people can vote on it. A referendum is a similar process, allowing voters to get rid of an existing law.

Riverboat gambling stirred up Missouri citizens in a recent example of the referendum process. According to Missouri's constitution, gambling can only be conducted on the Mississippi and Missouri Rivers. Some casinos created ponds next to the

Missouri River, connected to it by ditches or pipes, in order to comply with the law. They ran into trouble when the Missouri Supreme Court ruled that their artificial basins violated the constitution. When casino owners howled in complaint, the question of "boats in moats" was put to the people.

Supporters said that the casinos bring jobs to the community and pointed out that a percentage of the casinos' taxes supports the public schools. But opponents protested that the amount of money that actually goes to the schools is insignificant. "The total gambling tax dollars that support education in Missouri are equal to one textbook per child in Missouri," one reporter noted. They also objected that most of the casino jobs pay little more than the minimum wage. Furthermore, studies show that 5 percent of gamblers become addicted to gambling. Some lose their money, their jobs, and sometimes their families when they cannot stop gambling. "Gambling brings false hope, distress, . . . crime," stated Greg Holley, a St. Louis minister and ex-gambler. Some think casinos actually cost the state much more than they contribute, in bad debts, crime, and loss of income.

The casino industry spent almost $10 million to persuade voters to allow casinos in manmade basins. And 56 percent of the people who voted in the referendum said "yes," so the casinos stayed open.

THE ECONOMY OF ST. LOUIS

Luckily, gambling isn't the only way to make money in Missouri. There are plenty of jobs in manufacturing and service industries.

EARNING A LIVING

Manufacturing

- Airplanes
- Automobiles
- Chemicals
- Food products

Natural Resources

- Coal
- Lead
- Limestone

Agriculture

- Apples
- Beef cattle
- Corn
- Hogs
- Soybeans
- Turkeys

Cape Girardeau
Sikeston
Kennett
Poplar Bluff
West Plains
Park Hills
Rolla
St. Louis
Florissant
St. Charles
St. Peters
Washington
Fulton
Hannibal
Kirksville
Macon
Moberly
Columbia
Jefferson City
Sedalia
Trenton
Kansas City
Independence
Lees Summit
Marshall
Warrensburg
Nevada
Bolivar
Springfield
Branson
Neosho
Joplin
St. Joseph

Mississippi R.
St. Francis R.
Black R.
Current R.
Gasconade R.
Meramec R.
Missouri R.
Osage R.
Salt R.
N. Fork Salt R.
Mark Twain Lake
Chariton R.
Thompson R.
Grand R.
Platte R.
Smithville Reservoir
Lake of the Ozarks
South Grand R.
Harry S. Truman Reservoir
Pomme de Terre Lake
Horse R.
Stockton Lake
Spring R.
Table Rock Lake
Bull Shoals Lake
Wappapello Lake

Pb
L

GROSS STATE PRODUCT: $157 BILLION

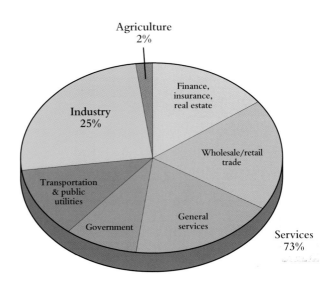

Agriculture
2%

Finance,
insurance,
real estate

Industry
25%

Wholesale/retail
trade

Transportation
& public
utilities

General
services

Government

Services
73%

(2000 estimated)

Much of the state's manufacturing is concentrated in or near its big cities, especially St. Louis.

Before Missouri was even a state St. Louis was already manufacturing shoes, furniture, pottery, bricks, and beer. By 1850, St. Louis was well established as an industrial center. In fact, after baseball became popular in the late 1800s, St. Louis was jokingly ranked "first in booze, first in shoes, and last in the American League."

Today's St. Louis retains much of its manufacturing legacy. Among its major industries are the Anheuser-Busch brewery, which produces almost half the beer consumed in the United States; the pet food producer Ralston-Purina; the airline TWA; and Boeing's military aircraft plant. Another important employer is the chemical company Monsanto, a pioneer in the development of genetically engineered crops, designed to resist diseases and pests.

But even with all these large companies, good jobs may not be easy to get. "Granted there is a record number of jobs in the country, but many workers need at least two of them to survive," noted William Kurtzeborn, a St. Louis area resident. This impression is confirmed by a recent study that showed that 79 percent of the fastest growing jobs in Missouri pay less than a livable wage for a family of four.

In fact, the city of St. Louis has become more and more impoverished over the past few decades. People and businesses moved out of the city to the surrounding suburbs, emptying it of taxpayers and commerce.

St. Louis is still a national leader in building fighter planes—but it doesn't make as many as it used to. When aircraft manufacturer Boeing announced layoffs in its St. Louis plant in 1999, almost seven thousand workers lost their jobs.

Formerly a city of industry, St. Louis is being eroded from the inside as residents leave for the cleaner, safer suburbs and companies leave for cheaper building rents.

In the suburbs, the prospects look much brighter. St. Charles County west of St. Louis was jubilant when the credit-card corporation MasterCard decided in 1999 to locate its Global Technology and Operations Center there. The telecommunications company MCI WorldCom soon followed, establishing a regional center there. "High-tech companies tend to cluster together," said Rick Finholt, director of the Missouri Research Park in St. Charles County. "Once you establish the cluster, others join."

Sure enough, in the 1990s, fifteen companies moved to the area.

Developers are optimistic about this high-tech economic expansion in the region west of St. Louis. "This is the direction growth is going in St. Louis," says Finholt. "We're in the path of growth."

MORE JOBS THAN WORKERS

In the 1990s, Kansas City also began to revive from economic hardships it had faced in the 1980s. Downtown office spaces filled up, and riverboat gambling brought a steady stream of tourists, which

Construction is one of the booming industries in Kansas City as the twenty-first century begins. Here, workers take an airy lunch break high above the city.

created a need for more hotels and restaurants. Low real estate prices persuaded large stores to build in the Kansas City area, and the city's improving economy motivated the restoration of older buildings downtown.

In recent years, Kansas City's low unemployment rate—around 4 percent—has generated higher incomes, more consumer spending, and new construction: in short, a thriving economy. It is only employers who are worried. "It used to be we could put an ad out for one job and get three hundred applications. Now an ad for ten jobs might only get a hundred applicants," says Gary O'Bannon, a human resources specialist for Kansas City.

Besides the casinos, big employers in the Kansas City area include grain processing companies, makers of pet foods, the greeting card company Hallmark, and Harley-Davidson motorcycles. But the biggest area of employment is the service industry, providing computer programming and jobs in hospitals, banks, sales, and telemarketing.

SMALL FARMS AND BIG PROBLEMS

"Agriculture is the bedrock of Missouri's economy," proclaimed state treasurer Bob Holden in 1998. Agriculture *was* the bedrock of Missouri's economy in the 1800s. The state still produces hogs, beef cattle, soybeans, and corn. But with the state's manufacturing and service economy on the rise, fewer and fewer Missourians are farmers. Large, high-production farms are also elbowing out small farmers, so that the family farm is rapidly becoming a thing of the past.

Harley-Davidson motorcycles are an American obsession. Harley fans consider them the king of motorcycles because of their size and power. Every year the Kansas City factory turns out hundreds of these glossy monsters.

These big farms are often combined with processing plants. For instance, many meatpacking companies own the hogs they process into pork. This means they buy fewer hogs from independent farmers. Since big factory farms make more money than small ones, they are better able to survive economic setbacks like low prices. Philip Martin, an independent hog farmer in Centralia, said pork prices have fallen to eighteen cents a pound, while it costs him

A DIFFERENT KIND OF LIVESTOCK

Farmers pushed out of hog, soybean, and corn farming by large producers sometimes turn to more specialized farming. Beekeeping, crayfish farming, and raising Christmas trees are some of the more unusual ways Missouri's small farmers are making a living.

Elk once roamed wild in Missouri, and they are coming back—except they're on farms. Terry Furstenau raises elk in Fayette. What started as a whim became a successful herd of fifty animals. Elk eat half as much feed as cattle, and they browse on native Missouri grasses. "It took more work to keep fifteen cattle alive during the winter than it did to keep fifty elk alive all year," calculated Furstenau.

He and others—about one hundred people in Missouri—raise elk not so much for their meat as for the velvet that grows on their antlers every year. The biggest market for this velvet is in Korea, where it is valued as a medicine.

Soybeans are one of the most important crops in Missouri's economy.

thirty-six cents a pound to raise a hog. "And you've still got to feed your family," he said.

Missouri lost five thousand independent farms between 1993 and 1999. One farmer lamented, "Rural America is dying. The way things are going, the only farmers left two years from now will be corporate farms and hobby farmers. . . . a way of life will disappear."

Another problem with giant farms is their environmental impact.

The sewage created by large hog farms is channeled into outdoor "lagoons." It is often improperly treated or contained, and sometimes leaks into the local water supply. In 1999, fifty-two enraged Missouri families won a lawsuit against the Continental Grain Company, one of the nation's largest producers of pork, for the horrible smell it produces. Described by a neighbor as "a devastating, ugly odor," the smell comes from bacteria in hog manure. Researchers are adding bacteria-killing substances to the manure to see if this will reduce the smell. Others suggest simply covering the lagoons. But "the sheer volume of manure produced by thousands of hogs is a real test for any lagoon," said Dennis Sievers, an agricultural engineer at the University of Missouri. "You can't just flush away your problems."

4
MIDDLE AMERICANS

Missouri is smack the middle of the country—sort of. At least, it's caught in the middle. Sandwiched between distinct regions of the United States, it shares regional traits with the states it rubs shoulders with. At one time, St. Louis stood for the industrial East and Kansas City for the Wild West. Today, St. Louis is still full of manufacturing and Kansas City is still a huge grain and livestock market, but the stereotypes of the past have mellowed and blended into a friendly mix.

THE STATE OF THE STATE

About 87 percent of Missourians are white and 11 percent are black. The other 2 percent are people of Asian, Pacific Island, Native Americans, and Hispanic heritage. More than half of Missourians live in urban areas, and the number of people living on farms is rapidly declining. City dwellers are moving to suburbs, and newcomers to Missouri tend to move to its popular recreational areas, especially around the beautiful Lake of the Ozarks region.

IMMIGRANTS, OLD AND NEW

The first Europeans to settle in what is now Missouri were French. They began building towns in the region in the eighteenth century,

Kids cool off in the spray of an open fire hydrant on a hot St. Louis summer day.

when it was still French territory. Ste. Genevieve, founded in 1735, was Missouri's first permanent European settlement. A big event in Ste. Genevieve today is the French Heritage Festival in May, with traditional music and an emphasis on the town's eighteenth-century French colonial history. "Why do people traipse to Williamsburg [Virginia] when there is such wonderful colonial history here?" asks Carl J. Ekberg, an expert on the local French architecture. According to Ekberg, Ste. Genevieve has more French buildings than New Orleans, Louisiana, a city famous for its charming French district.

ETHNIC MISSOURI

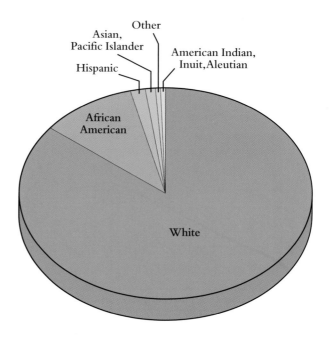

Other

Asian,
Pacific Islander

Hispanic

American Indian,
Inuit, Aleutian

African
American

White

By the early nineteenth century, Missouri belonged to the United States. Its factories were booming, and people were needed to work in them. As Europeans heard about the jobs available in Missouri, they began coming in great waves, to escape poverty, hunger, and political and religious intolerance in their native countries.

The largest number of immigrants in the mid-1800s came from Germany. Towns with names like New Hamburg, Schubert, and Frankenstein show their Germanic roots. By 1850, almost a third of the population of St. Louis was German.

Other Germans came to farm the cheap land. Hermann, a town in a lush river valley about forty-five miles west of St. Louis, was settled during the heavy German immigration between 1830 and 1870. Many German farmers grew fruits and berries, especially grapes and apples. The soil was excellent for grape growing, and the town became known for its excellent German wines. Oktoberfest is a celebration of this German heritage. It is held every weekend in October in Hermann, when people get together to taste the local wines, eat their fill of hearty German food, and get an earful of authentic German music.

In the late 1800s, people began arriving in Missouri from Ireland, Scotland, Belgium, Wales, Switzerland, Portugal, Italy, and Czechoslovakia. A lack of jobs in Italy in the 1880s brought a flood of immigrants to the St. Louis area. By the mid-1890s the St. Louis neighborhood that came to be called the Hill was almost entirely Italian. Many Italians who had worked in clay mines in Italy took jobs in St. Louis's brick factories or in nearby clay, lead, and coal mines. This neighborhood is where Lawrence "Yogi" Berra grew up. Berra was a baseball player legendary for his amusing sayings, like "If people don't want to come out to the ball park, you can't stop 'em."

Today, Missouri's immigrant population is not huge, but it's getting larger, especially in St. Louis. Since the 1970s, St. Louis has received a stream of Vietnamese immigrants. Other southeast Asians, from Thailand, Laos, and the Philippines, have also come to the city. Today the community around South Grand Boulevard is full of Asian and Hispanic restaurants, grocery stores, and bakeries.

St. Louis's growing Mexican community is centered in the neighborhood of Cherokee and Iowa Streets. Three of the nearby Catholic churches offer mass in Spanish. Mexican, Vietnamese, Ethiopian, and white kids mix at a local Catholic school. Mexican grocery stores and restaurants fill the red brick buildings of this neighborhood. There is even a Mexican cowboy clothing store! In

In the late 1800s, many Italians moved to
St. Louis. Most settled on the Hill, which is
still a thriving Italian neighborhood.

Today's immigrants to St. Louis include more
and more people from Southeast Asia. Here, a
family enjoys watching the annual Japanese
Festival.

Mexicans are another growing group of recent arrivals to Missouri. Here, a Mexican family shares a meal in Kansas City.

1998, the community celebrated its first Cinco de Mayo festival—
a Mexican holiday—with hopes of many more to come.

BARBECUE AND THEN SOME

Kansas City has been called the Barbecue Capital of the World. Two
things make Kansas City barbecue sauce distinctive. One is the
addition of vinegar for tanginess. The other, according to barbecue
fan Rich Davis, is its combination of tomato sauce and hot pepper
"with molasses for character and body, not just sweetness."

One of the city's most famous barbecue restaurants is Arthur
Bryant's. Writer and Kansas City native Calvin Trillin titled it "the
single best restaurant in the world." American presidents have
eaten there. One barbecue enthusiast reported, "On the day I was
there, I saw cars from twelve states" in the parking lot. On the wall
of the restaurant is a newspaper cartoon. Arthur Bryant himself is
standing at the pearly gates of heaven and Saint Peter asks him,
"Did you bring any sauce?"

Other parts of the state have their own specialties. St. Louis is
famous for its Italian restaurants and superb frozen custard. At a
place called Ted Drewe's, this ice cream–type dessert is so thick
that St. Louisians call it a "concrete." The Ozark region is
renowned for its down-home cuisine of "close-to-the-earth foods."
The area's abundant fish, game, herbs, and fruit have produced
local delicacies such as apple dumplings and catfish fried in corn-
bread batter. "This is the kind of food grandma used to do on
Sundays," says Ozark chef Moose Zader.

All this good eating has its down side. Kansas City was ranked

KANSAS CITY BARBECUE SAUCE
ON CHICKEN DRUMSTICKS

This is the dish to serve when everybody wants the drumstick. (But you can also use a package of mixed chicken parts.) Have an adult help you with this recipe.

½ cup water
¼ cup cider vinegar
¼ cup molasses
¼ cup sugar
1 tablespoon mustard
1 teaspoon chili powder
1 teaspoon salt
4 cloves garlic, chopped fine
¼ cup soy sauce
8 ounces tomato sauce
package of 8 chicken drumsticks or mixed chicken parts

In a saucepan, combine all the ingredients but the chicken. Heat the pan on the stove over medium heat. Stir the sauce until it begins to boil, then turn down heat, and simmer for 20 minutes. When sauce is the thickness of ketchup, remove from heat and let cool.

Turn on the oven broiler. Rinse the chicken parts and lay them in the broiler. Broil for 25 minutes or until the meat inside is no longer pink. Pull out the broiler pan (careful—it's hot!). Baste the chicken with your barbecue sauce and broil for 5 more minutes exactly. If the sauce is cooked too long, it will get bitter. Arrange the chicken on a platter. Serve with mashed potatoes, cole slaw, and apple crisp.

the fourth most obese city in a national survey in 1997. Calvin Trillin, for one, was proud that his city had received such a distinction. "National recognition is always gratifying," he said. "And 'Fourth Fattest' does have a nice ring, whether or not they decide to put it on the city-limits signs."

CARDINALS, RAMS, ROYALS, AND CHIEFS

Every state loves their sports teams—no matter how bad—and Missouri is no exception. St. Louis's former baseball team the St.

Mark McGwire's powerful swing earned him the title Baseball's Home Run King. Here he hits another home run for the St. Louis Cardinals.

Louis Browns was a terrible team for years and years. They finally made it to the World Series in 1944, but only because all the best players in the league were off fighting in World War II. In 1954, the Browns moved to Baltimore and became the Orioles—and a much better team.

St. Louis still has a baseball team, the Cardinals. In 1997, slugger Mark McGwire joined the team. The following year, he began hitting the ball out of the park with astonishing regularity. McGwire was soon on a pace to break the single-season record of sixty-one home runs set by Roger Maris in 1961. Fans came to games three hours early just to watch him at batting practice, and toward the end of the season every game was sold out. McGwire ended up smashing Maris's record by hitting seventy home runs.

Missouri is also home to baseball's Kansas City Royals and football's Kansas City Chiefs and St. Louis Rams.

SUMMER FUN

But Missourians don't just like watching sports, however spectacular. They also like getting out and having some fun themselves. Lake of the Ozarks is one of the most popular destinations, an ideal spot for boating, waterskiing, swimming, and fishing.

Every Memorial Day, Lake of the Ozarks is mobbed with boaters—up to 40,000 of them. And people keep coming all summer. But when a horde of boats that big is combined with alcohol and lax safety precautions, boating fun turns dangerous. "There are people who come down here with more horsepower than brains," attests Stacey Mosher, a Missouri Water Patrol officer.

In 1997, Missouri ranked fourth in the nation for serious boating accidents, with 333 accidents and 25 deaths. More than half of these accidents occurred at Lake of the Ozarks.

Many blame the problem on Missouri's relaxed boating laws. For instance, jet skis accounted for 30 percent of boating accidents in the state in 1997. Soon after that, Missouri passed a law raising the minimum age for operating them from twelve to fourteen, and the number of accidents dropped 28 percent.

So laws do work; it's just that Missourians don't like having a lot of laws. Missouri is unlike many other states in that no one is obliged to take boat-operating, swimming, or basic water safety classes. "Some people have no respect for what boats can do," said Mosher. "They think the worst thing that can happen is they get wet. They don't think about running into the side of a boat on their jet ski." In Missouri it is legal to drink alcohol and drive a boat. Also, state law requires only that adults have life jackets in the boat, not that they wear them. "Trying to get adults to wear life jackets is a real struggle," laments Ruth Wood of the BOAT/US Safety Foundation. Boater Kenny Carroll affirms, "When you're on a boat, you want to be wearing nothing but shorts."

FAIRS AND FESTIVALS

The prairie town of Sedalia fills with happy revelers every August. It is the proud host of the Missouri State Fair, offering carnival rides, tractor pulls, and barbecue contests. The livestock shows don't just feature cows and horses; now they include llamas and dogs. "We've really put in a concerted effort to give everyone a great show," said

Lake of the Ozarks is a vacationer's paradise, with its fishing and boating opportunities. The lake's many little inlets give it a tremendously long shoreline —1,500 miles!

Kim Allen, marketing director for the fair. This is clear from the new events they've added to attract more visitors, such as alligator wrestling and high-diving acrobats.

But the state fair is not the only fair in Missouri, not by a long shot. The state is brimming with fairs and festivals honoring

TELL ME A STORY

A steely, chilling voice warns you that something is "a' slippin', a' slidin', a' inchin'" up behind you. What do you do? Shudder and then laugh. It's only a story. But it transfixes listeners today, just as it did in the Missouri of yesteryear, when storytelling was a major form of entertainment on cold winter evenings.

Today, the folk tradition of storytelling is kept alive at the St. Louis Storytelling Festival, held in May. It is hugely popular with both kids and adults. "This is better than videos because you make the pictures in your head," comments third-grader Shelby Boston.

"It's a way of connecting with who we are, why we're here and where we've come from," says Ron Turner, one of the festival's founders. "That's why 20,000 to 25,000 people stop what they're doing and go and sit and listen to another human being." Local storyteller Sylvia Duncan remarks, "People say you're crazy. You're going to stand up there with nothing but your voice and keep a hundred children entertained? But you do."

Missouri's cultural and historical heritage and its natural bounty and recreational pleasures.

For starters, Sedalia boasts the Scott Joplin Ragtime Festival in June, where lively music takes you back to the turn of the century. You can find a festival for just about any type of music in Missouri. The St. Louis Big Muddy Blues and Roots Festival, offering blues, rock, swing, and jazz, is held in September. The Lake of the Ozarks Dogwood Festival, held in April to coincide with the blooming of dogwood trees, offers bluegrass music, arts and crafts, and carnival rides. Kansas City's Public Festival celebrates the area's black musical history with jazz concerts.

Bluegrass music is alive and well in concerts and festivals across the state, from the Ozarks to St. Louis to Kansas City.

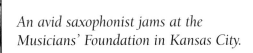

An avid saxophonist jams at the Musicians' Foundation in Kansas City.

Another Kansas City annual event—perhaps the oldest one—is the American Royal Livestock, Horse Show and Rodeo, held during the first two weeks in November, honoring Kansas City's history as a cattle market and cowboy town.

And who could forget food as a reason for celebrating! Kansas City is almost synonymous with barbecue, and it has the festivals to prove it. At least a dozen Kansas City Barbecue Society "sanctioned events" are held throughout the state, including the Jesse James BBQ Cook-Out held in Kearney (James's birthplace) in September. The Strawberry Festival in Bridgeton in early June has a quilt and craft auction, a children's carnival, craft demonstrations, and local delicacies—including, of course, strawberry pie, strawberry shortcake, and best of all, fresh strawberries.

"WE ALWAYS LIE TO STRANGERS"

Another type of Missouri fun is telling tall tales. The Ozark hill country has a long history of this kind of storytelling. The Ozarks are famed for lagging behind the rest of the country in cultural and technological change. Vance Randolph, a collector of Ozark folklore, calls the people of the Ozarks "the most deliberately unprogressive people in the United States." One story tells of the inhabitants of Bates County, who in the mid-1800s were terrified by the whistle of the *Flora Jones*, the first steamboat to go up the Osage River. They thought it was the scream of a "super-panther."

The region's isolated valleys, combined with bad roads and self-sufficient living, helped people in the Ozarks maintain their language and customs. This isolation bred a contempt for the out-

THE LUCKY SHOT

The typical Ozark tall tale features a hunter who is incredibly lucky or skillful. Here is a story where luck is hard at work.

A hunter was out hunting with a double-barreled shotgun when he saw a rabbit and fired at it. Just as he fired, the rabbit ran into a flock of partridges, and with the shot from one barrel the hunter killed the rabbit and eleven partridges. The sound of the shot scared a turkey out of hiding, and as it flew up into the trees the hunter shot it with the other barrel. The dead turkey fell into the branches of a tree, and while the hunter was getting it down, he found a huge beehive full of honey. Walking home with his prizes, he sighted another rabbit. He had forgotten to reload, so he threw his gun at the rabbit and killed it. When he went to pick up the rabbit and the gun, he fell through a rotten plank covering an underground treasure.

side world. The Ozark expression "never trust a fellow that wears a suit" reflects a prejudice against people from big cities. Ozarkians sometimes showed the same prejudice toward anyone they didn't know personally, as demonstrated in another local expression, "we always lie to strangers."

Despite the invasion of modern life in the form of automobiles and television, some traditional folk arts, like fiddle playing, quilt making, and wood carving, have survived. So has the tendency to tell folk tales that are amusing, vivid, and usually unbelievable. In the 1930s and 1940s, there was even a club of old pranksters called the Post, whose "sole purpose was playing jokes on strangers and

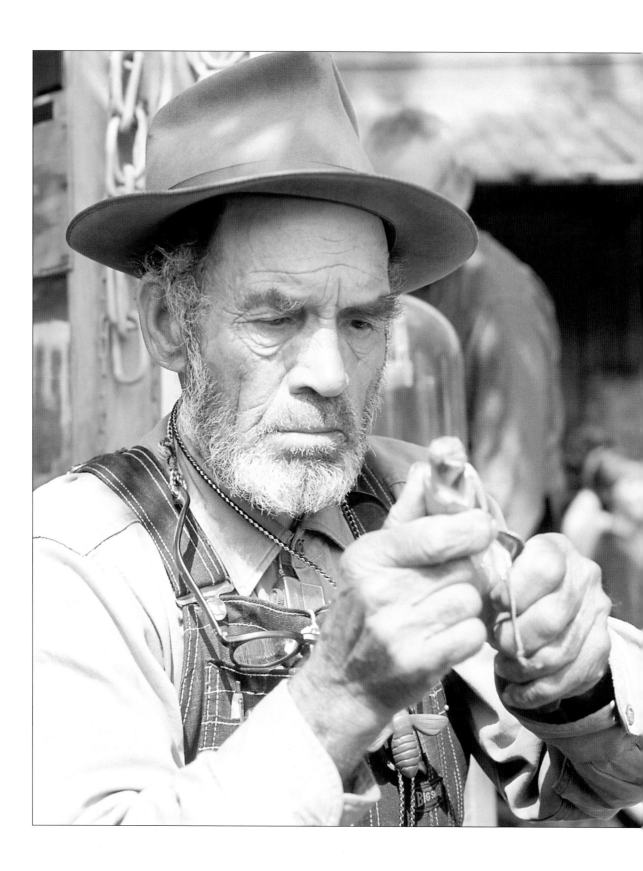

making them believe outrageous falsehoods," says Randolph.

Missouri tall tales frequently have to do with the plentiful hunting and fishing opportunities in the Ozarks' valleys and forests. Stories of outrunning wolves, killing bears with a jackknife, shooting one hundred ducks with one load of shot—anything is possible says writer Frederick Simpich. "They don't expect you to believe, but they do like you to laugh and appreciate their story-telling powers."

A man carves a corncob pipe at a crafts festival in Branson. Other old-fashioned crafts survive in the Ozarks, like making furniture, pottery, and quilts by hand.

5 A WEALTH OF TALENT

Missouri has given birth to scientists, writers, painters, musicians, poets, and politicians. The state's finest heroes have learned from its land, portrayed its people in words and paint, created new music, and farmed richness out of its sometimes rocky terrain.

RAGTIME INNOVATOR

Composer Scott Joplin was born in Texas in 1868, but as a youth he traveled up and down the Mississippi Valley, doing odd jobs and playing the piano in bars. Eventually he settled in Sedalia, Missouri, where he studied harmony and composition in college and became a dedicated musician.

At the time, ragtime was a general term for the kind of piano music played in saloons. Its roots were a mix of African rhythms, European dances like polkas, and marching band music. Joplin took this mixture and developed it into a distinctive style of music. While keeping the "ragged time" the music was named for, he created a sophisticated, precise form. Arthur Marshall, a friend of Joplin's, said, "Rags were played in Sedalia before Scott Joplin settled there, but he got to making them really go."

It was in Sedalia that Joplin began writing and publishing his original works. His "Maple Leaf Rag," named after a club where he often played, was published in 1899. It was the first piece of

At the Scott Joplin Ragtime Festival in Sedalia, the sound of ragtime music is heard everywhere. "Visitors, helplessly moved by its buoyant beat, kick up their heels and dance," writes reporter Barbara Noe.

American music to sell more than one million copies. The mania for ragtime peaked over the next five years, with families and friends gathering around the parlor piano in the evenings to play the latest rags. And it was those by Joplin, the first famous black musician in America, against which all others were measured.

THE FATHER OF MODERN AGRICULTURE

By the end of his life, George Washington Carver was a pioneer in soil and crop chemistry, but the beginning of his life was rather grim.

George Washington Carver only patented three of his five hundred agricultural inventions. He said, "God gave them to me, how can I sell them to someone else?" Here, Carver teaches soil analysis in a lab at the Tuskegee Institute in Alabama.

George was born on a farm in Diamond Grove in 1864, the son of slaves. After he was orphaned, he was raised by a white couple.

George often helped his foster mother with housework. By the time he was ten he could cook, make candles and soap, and design and sew patchwork quilts. But the thing he did best was making things grow. Mrs. Carver's garden was admired for miles around. George took care of the plants, many of which he had transplanted from nearby fields and woods.

As a youth Carver traveled, always pursuing his education. He settled down at Iowa State College in Ames, where he studied botany and agricultural chemistry. In 1896, he moved to Tuskegee, Alabama, to teach at a school for black students. The director of Tuskegee Institute, Booker T. Washington, had heard of Carver's work and his ability to "raise corn on a wooden floor."

In his research, Carver had found that some plants add nutrients to the soil they grow in. Other plants use up nutrients and leave the soil exhausted, especially if the same crop is planted several years in a row. On this principle, Carver advised farmers to plant peanuts and sweet potatoes, and not to plant cotton all the time. But most farmers kept planting cotton because of its high prices. Only after a hungry insect called the boll weevil destroyed their cotton crops did farmers take Carver's advice.

Carver also developed more than three hundred new products in his laboratory, all made from peanuts and sweet potatoes. He created soap, ink, shaving cream, linoleum, shampoo, and beverages—imagine drinking sweet potato milk in peanut coffee!—but his most famous invention was peanut butter.

THE FIRST PUBLIC KINDERGARTEN

Educational reformer Susan Elizabeth Blow was raised in a comfortable home in Carondolet, Missouri. She had the usual upbringing of an upper-middle-class girl, made up of irregular schooling, reading the Bible, learning French from her governess, teaching her younger siblings, and being sent to "finishing school" in the East. When she was a young woman she traveled with her family to Europe.

"GIVE 'EM HELL, HARRY!"

Harry S. Truman, the only Missourian to become president, got a reputation early in life for hard work and determination. An artillery captain during World War I, he returned home after the war and managed a hat shop in Kansas City. When the shop failed, Truman turned to politics and was elected a judge. He was elected to the U.S. Senate in 1934, where he became known for his common sense.

During World War II, President Franklin D. Roosevelt chose Truman as his vice president. But Roosevelt died less than three months after beginning his fourth term in office. So in April 1945, in the heat of the war, Harry Truman was sworn in as the new president of the United States.

Truman's critics thought he would be an ineffectual president, because he was not a colorful speaker or a cultured statesman. But Truman proved to be popular and capable. He was valued for his honesty, and his plain style of speaking grew on America. In his 1948 campaign speeches, his criticisms of Congress drew shouts of "Give 'em hell, Harry!" Truman replied, "I don't give 'em hell. I just tell the truth and they think it's hell."

When the 1948 presidential election rolled around, experts believed that Truman's Republican opponent, Thomas Dewey, would win. Dewey's optimistic but vague campaign speeches seemed to sugarcoat America's problems in an appealing way. But against all expectation, Truman won. Harry had "given 'em hell," and the American people wanted him back.

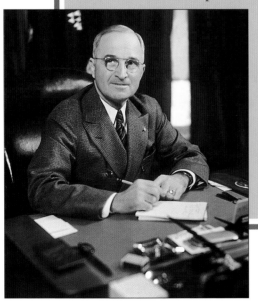

Susan Blow helped to change drab, somber schoolrooms into pleasant places to learn and play. Today at the Susan E. Blow Center in St. Louis, teachers and students reenact the original games and activities of the first kindergarten.

In Germany the educational theories of Friedrich Froebel caught her interest. Froebel believed that young children learned through games and play. He urged teachers to encourage creativity and self-expression in children—a new idea at the time. Childrens' activities should focus on cultural and spiritual enrichment, not just on practical lessons. It was Froebel who invented the word *kindergarten*—a garden of children.

When Blow returned to St. Louis, she put Froebel's ideas into practice, opening the first public kindergarten in the United States in 1873. Her schoolroom was cheerfully decorated. Her method included time to play. She taught children in the morning, and in the afternoon she trained teachers, who started kindergartens throughout the country. Ten years later, every St. Louis public school had a kindergarten. Thanks to Blow's teachings, kindergarten became an important part of American education.

PAINTING THE PEOPLE AND THE LAND

Born in Neosho, in southwestern Missouri, painter Thomas Hart Benton had some big expectations to live up to. He had been named after his great-uncle, a forceful U.S. senator. His father, a lawyer and local politician, hoped young Tom would follow in the family footsteps and go into politics and law. But Tom was not

Thomas Hart Benton's paintings and murals are distinctive for their earthy, vigorous images of working people. In the words of art critic Robert Hughes, Benton's paintings celebrate "the heroism of work."

interested. He didn't care for school. He preferred roaming the countryside, getting in fights—and drawing.

When he was a boy, Benton traveled extensively with his politician father. The farmers, railroad workers, and builders he saw made a deep impression on him. He liked the rawness and strength of people who worked for a living physically, whose bodies were always in a kind of struggle with the earth. His paintings show how he saw the American landscape: flowing, dynamic, and muscular. Not just the men but also the women; and not just the people but the land. Even his paintings of hills and trees look muscular!

His style was scornfully called "regionalism," as if to say nobody from the outside world could like his work. His paintings and murals were criticized for portraying ordinary people, scenes of people gambling, dancing, brawling, and even robbing trains. These were considered unacceptable subjects for paintings in a time when art was supposed to be noble, uplifting, and civilized.

But Benton ignored these criticisms and kept on painting life the way he saw it. Two of his best-known murals are in the state capitol in Jefferson City, Missouri, and in the Truman Library in Independence, Missouri.

PIONEER WRITER

As a young woman, beloved children's author Laura Ingalls Wilder moved to Missouri, where she lived the rest of her life. Originally from Wisconsin, her family had moved frequently looking for good farmland. Even when they found it, droughts and swarms of grasshoppers often destroyed their crops.

As she traveled into Missouri, Laura Ingalls Wilder wrote, "The farther we go, the more we like this country. . . . The distances and the valleys are blue. . . . It is a drowsy country that makes you feel wide awake and alive but somehow contented."

When Laura Ingalls married Almanzo Wilder, they too tried to make a success of farming, but low wheat prices, illness, and debt frustrated their hopes. In 1894, they moved south with their daughter, Rose, hoping to find a better life in the Ozarks orchard country, or as the Missouri real estate ads called it, "the land of the Big Red Apple."

They found it in Mansfield, Missouri, where they bought forty acres and built a house. This is the house where Laura wrote her famous "Little House" books about her frontier childhood, and where Rose grew up, also to become a writer. Even though she was doing much of the farmwork, Laura became a respected columnist

MARK TWAIN: RIVERBOAT PILOT

Missouri native Samuel Clemens, alias Mark Twain, is best known as the author of *The Adventures of Tom Sawyer* and *The Adventures of Huckleberry Finn*. But he was not just a writer. Throughout his life he had many jobs, and he spent several years as a riverboat pilot on the Mississippi River. He even took his name, Mark Twain, from a term used to measure the depth of the river: "mark twain" was short for "marking two fathoms." Some of his most powerful writing comes from his experiences on the river, where he learned the language of the water and what it meant to the people who traveled on it:

> The face of the water, in time, became a wonderful book . . . it had a new story to tell every day. . . . The passenger who could not read it was charmed with a peculiar sort of faint dimple on its surface; but to the pilot . . . it meant that a wreck or a rock was buried there that could tear the life out of the strongest vessel that ever floated. . . . In truth, the passenger who could not read this book saw nothing but all manner of pretty pictures in it, painted by the sun and shaded by the clouds.

for the local paper, writing practical articles about farming and politics.

In one of these articles, she wrote about how hard it was to scratch a living from the rocky land. As Laura wrote, "When I look at the farm now and see the smooth, green, rolling meadows and pastures, the good fields of corn and wheat . . . I can hardly bring back to my mind the rough, rocky, brushy, ugly place that we first called Rocky Ridge Farm. The name given it then serves to remind us of the battles we have fought and won."

A SAXOPHONIST CALLED BIRD

His music was called "inhuman" and "absurd" by critics, but Charlie Parker, who was nicknamed Bird, changed the definition of jazz. Growing up in Kansas City, Missouri, Charlie spent his boyhood hanging around nightclubs. He learned from listening to great horn players like Herschel Evans and Lester Young.

Charlie started playing saxophone in high school. At fourteen, he was tall for his age, so he was able to get into clubs without attracting attention. There he studied the music scene, the bands and soloists. When Parker was nineteen he moved to New York City. He began playing with famous musicians like trumpeter Dizzy Gillespie and pianist Thelonius Monk. They began to forge a new sound called bebop. Bebop was jerky and full of rapidly climbing and falling notes. It was rhythmically bizarre and difficult to play. Parker took it over and created a jazz that few could understand and nobody else could play.

Just about everyone who heard him play agreed that Bird was a genius. But he had become addicted to heroin, and this addiction ate into his life. He borrowed money from friends and strangers, and often would pawn his saxophone to get cash to buy drugs. He showed up late for practice and for jobs—or didn't show up at all. One night he was even banned from Birdland, a jazz club named in his honor.

Parker died at age thirty-four, having ruined his health with alcohol and drugs. But he left behind a bebop legacy and established the saxophone as the main instrument of jazz for decades to come. One of his fans said: "Bird was like a lit match in a beaker of pure oxygen: burns out quickly but, oh! how brightly!"

One day when Charlie Parker and some friends were driving in the country, their car hit a chicken that had wandered into the road. Charlie said to the driver, "Hey man, did you know you hit that yard bird back there?" After that, all his friends called him Yardbird, or just Bird.

6 SHOW ME MISSOURI!

Travelers to Missouri find that there is plenty to see in the Show Me State. From a living butterfly museum to the tallest monument in the United States, Missouri boasts a marvelous assortment of treats.

MARK TWAIN'S BOYHOOD HOME

Hannibal is a sleepy town on the Mississippi River. Two things put it on the map: the riverboat trade and the writing of Mark Twain. This is the town where Twain grew up, and it forms the background for his books *The Adventures of Tom Sawyer* and *The Adventures of Huckleberry Finn*.

Today, the town retains much of the nineteenth-century feeling of its heyday. You can enjoy a ride on the *Mark Twain* riverboat, steaming down the Mississippi on an hour-long cruise full of history and folklore. Or join the crowd in July for National Tom Sawyer Days, featuring fence-whitewashing and frog-jumping contests. Then head downriver to even more historic St. Louis.

GATEWAY TO THE WEST

Countless pioneers passed through St. Louis on their way into the heart of wild America. The gleaming Gateway Arch is a monument to the city's role as Gateway to the West. It stands at the river's edge, a 630-foot-tall arc of shining steel, with the Mississippi to the east and downtown St. Louis to the west.

The impressive thirty-mile view from the top of the arch is well worth the ride up. Visitors clamber into a small egg-shaped capsule, which is pulled to the top of the curve inside one of its hollow "legs." The riders hear a loud cranking noise like that of a roller coaster

This boy hopes his frog is a winner in the frog-jumping contest, a regular event at Tom Sawyer Days every July in Hannibal. The contest is based on the Mark Twain story "The Celebrated Jumping Frog of Calaveras County."

St. Louis's elegant Gateway Arch was designed by architect Eero Saarinen. He got the idea for its shape while he was playfully spinning a thin metal chain in the air.

being pulled up its first big hill. It's unnerving to actually hear the machinery when you are used to the smooth silence of regular elevators. Each capsule seats five people—snugly. But even if five total strangers get in, they often emerge laughing and talking after their unusual ride.

One of the greatest things about St. Louis is Forest Park, because it has so much in it besides trees and green spaces. It has the St. Louis Zoo, the St. Louis Science Center, the St. Louis Art Museum, and the Missouri History Museum—all free. "Forest Park is the one place that everybody in St. Louis thinks they own," says Caitlin McQuade, curator at the Missouri Historical Society Museum.

On the zoo grounds stands a fantastic ironwork aviary, a relic of

The science center at Forest Park is full of fascinating exhibits that challenge the imagination.

the 1904 world's fair. Inside it, humans can wander amidst the birds and vegetation.

The science center features a planetarium, a life-size Tyrannosaurus rex that moves and roars, and a specially designed room where kids can be shaken by imitation earthquakes. It also offers displays that invite kids to practice surgery and to use police radar to clock the speeds of cars on the interstate highway.

TEN LARGEST CITIES

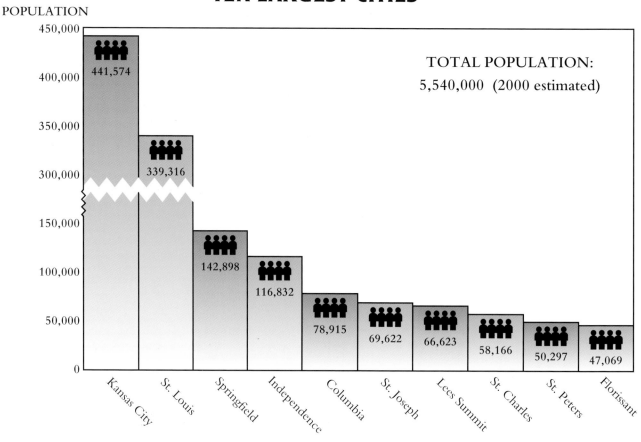

POPULATION

TOTAL POPULATION:
5,540,000 (2000 estimated)

Kansas City 441,574
St. Louis 339,316
Springfield 142,898
Independence 116,832
Columbia 78,915
St. Joseph 69,622
Lees Summit 66,623
St. Charles 58,166
St. Peters 50,297
Florissant 47,069

At Elephant Rocks State Park, "There's these enormous pink rocks, in the middle of nowhere, all piled on top of each other. It would obviously be a sacred place for somebody," comments Missourian David Goodman.

MASTODONS AND PETROGLYPHS

South of St. Louis, in Imperial, is Mastodon State Historic Site. There you can find the fossilized bones of mastodons, elephant-like beasts with enormous tusks. Washington State Park, in De Soto, is known for its petroglyphs, symbols carved into rock by prehistoric people.

Another geological attraction is Elephant Rocks State Park, near

Graniteville, where you can climb around on billion-year-old boulders. They don't look like elephants; they're as big as elephants. "They look like giant softballs," says John Meyer, who grew up nearby.

THE CAVE STATE

Amidst the Ozarks' wooded hills are hundreds of limestone caves, many filled with spectacular rock formations. These shapes are created by water slowly dripping through the soft limestone rock, like moisture creeping through a sponge. This water carries minerals from the limestone. As the water drips through the ceilings of the caves, the minerals slowly build up into solid forms. Some of these formations are quite fantastic, resembling frozen waterfalls, enormous forkfuls of spaghetti, or towers of stacked jellyfish. The most impressive caves attract thousands of visitors every year.

Meramec Caverns in Stanton might be the best known of Missouri's caves. Inside, it looks like cascades of yellow, gray, and white foam have poured down the walls and turned to stone. In places, these stone ridges look like tall curtains. Stalagmites stick up from the floor like fingers, while icicle-shaped stalactites point down from the ceiling. Some caves contain whole eerie forests of knobby columns.

Meramec Caverns is famed for its weird and breathtaking rock formations. Legend has it that in the 1870s, the famous outlaw Jesse James hid inside these caves after a train robbery, with his gang and all their horses.

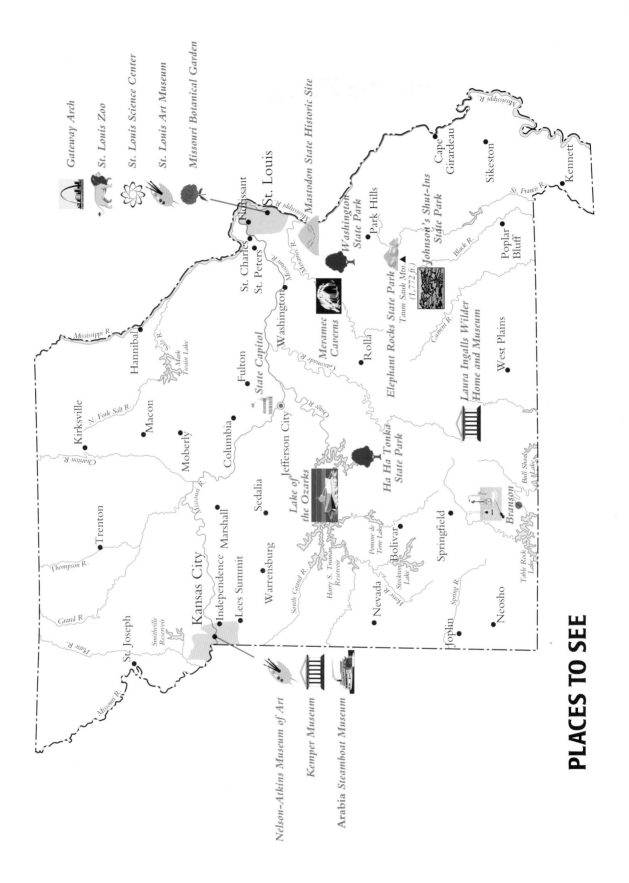

Gateway Arch
St. Louis Zoo
St. Louis Science Center
St. Louis Art Museum
Missouri Botanical Garden

St. Louis
Florissant
Mastodon State Historic Site

Mississippi R.
Mississippi R.
Cape Girardeau
Sikeston
Kennett
St. Francis R.

St. Charles
St. Peters
Washington State Park
Park Hills
Poplar Bluff

Missouri R.
Meramec R.

Washington
Meramec Caverns
Elephant Rocks State Park
Taum Sauk Mtn. ▲ (1,772 ft.)
Johnson's Shut-Ins State Park
Black R.

State Capitol
Rolla
Current R.
West Plains

Gasconade R.

Hannibal
Salt R.
Mark Twain Lake
Fulton
Laura Ingalls Wilder Home and Museum

Mississippi R.
N. Fork Salt R.
Kirksville
Macon
Columbia
Jefferson City
Osage R.

Chariton R.
Moberly
Lake of the Ozarks
Ha Ha Tonka State Park

Bull Shoals Lake

Trenton
Sedalia
Branson
Springfield

Thompson R.
Marshall
Warrensburg
Pomme de Terre Lake
Bolivar
Stockton Lake
Table Rock Lake

Kansas City
Independence
Lees Summit
South Grand R.
Harry S. Truman Reservoir
Horse Lake
Nevada
Neosho

Grand R.
St. Joseph
Smithville Reservoir
Joplin
Spring R.

Platte R.
Missouri R.

Nelson-Atkins Museum of Art
Kemper Museum
Arabia Steamboat Museum

PLACES TO SEE

NEON AND HAY BALES

If you like dazzling musical shows with lots of glitter, head south-west to Branson, which boasts of more live country music and variety shows than Nashville, Tennessee. Branson has long been a resort town, drawing visitors to its rivers and lakes. But today the main reason people flock to Branson is its over-the-top musical productions.

For instance, at Dixie Stampede, guests sit down to a lavish dinner while watching a mock Civil War battle set to music. In it, Union and Confederate "soldiers" on thirty-two horses clash in a "friendly North-South rivalry." Warm-up acts include trick horse-back riding and ostrich races.

Most of Branson's theaters are clustered along its main street, known as the Strip. Even before night falls, the Strip is lit up with neon and colored lights spelling out the names of its show palaces, where country music stars like Kenny Rogers perform. About seven million people a year visit Branson.

If you're tired from sitting during all those shows, journalist Doug Serven recommends Doennig's Sport Swings, about twenty miles north of Branson. Visitors grab onto ropes attached to the rafters of a barn, and jump off stacked bales of hay to swing through the air. "Sounds stupid, but it's a blast," reports Serven. "Uncontrolled yelling is encouraged."

LAKE OF THE OZARKS

In the center of the state is the beautiful Lake of the Ozarks. This gigantic lake is a popular summer attraction for boaters and jet

skiers, and its many small inlets are perfect quiet spots for fishing
or canoeing. You might also want to drift lazily down the winding
Osage River as it passes between magnificent limestone bluffs
crowned with groves of trees.

At Ha Ha Tonka State Park, a ruined castle looks out over the
lake. At the end of the nineteenth century, Kansas City millionaire
Robert McClure Snyder visited the area. He loved its limestone

*Businessman Robert Snyder chose the site for his sixty-room mansion because
of its lovely view of the surrounding woods and bluffs. Unfortunately, he died
in a car accident before his "castle" was ever built.*

bluffs and oak and hickory forests, so he built his dream house there in the style of a European castle. Time has ravaged the castle—in 1942 a fire burned out the insides—but the outer walls still stand. Visitors can admire the ruin and enjoy the spectacular view of the wooded cliffs and streams.

Near Lake of the Ozarks, in Osage Beach, is a very specialized zoo: it has only butterflies. Hank Weinmeister's House of Butterflies, an enclosure with twenty types of butterflies loose inside, invites you to wander among them and let them land on your hand. Chat with the owner for inside information, enjoy the atmospheric music, and have a slice of cake in the tea room.

KANSAS CITY, HERE I COME

"Who in Europe, or in America for that matter, knows that Kansas City is one of the loveliest cities on earth?" asked writer Andre Maurois.

Kansas City is indeed a hidden treasure. Although it is well known for its barbecue and jazz, few people realize it also has more fountains than any city in the world except Rome, Italy. It is home to two excellent art museums and a surprising assortment of public sculpture.

The Nelson-Atkins Museum of Art has one of the finest collections of Asian art in the world, and a sculpture garden featuring a dozen works by Henry Moore, who created large, abstract forms of the human body. You can also see some surprising art before you even enter the museum. On the spacious green lawn in front of this state-ly stone building, four huge red-and-white badminton birdies lie

JAZZ REBORN

Kansas City is enjoying a revival. Back in the 1930s, music clubs rocked and jumped with the playing of jazz greats like Count Basie and Charlie Parker. The jazz scene has dwindled over the decades, but new life is being breathed into it today.

This rebirth includes improving the city's neglected downtown area and restoring the once-famous jazz club district. The city has built the American Jazz Museum, the Gem Theater, and the Negro Leagues Baseball Museum to attract jazz lovers and tourists to the area, and they expect nightclubs and restaurants to follow.

The restoration has aroused some controversy, though. Some citizens felt that money was being thrown away on a project that would not last, in a run-down part of town. And Kansas City mayor Emanuel Cleaver was criticized when he spent $140,000 in public money on a clear plastic saxophone!

But this was a very special saxophone. It was the one Charlie Parker played in the 1953 Massey Hall concert in Toronto, Canada—which some music lovers claim was the greatest jazz concert ever. Many Kansas Citians now feel the price was worth it. That piece of jazz history has added a unique flavor to the museum. At the grand opening, actor Harry Belafonte said, "There's obviously a history here that refuses to pass. It endures."

scattered. It looks like some careless, gigantic badminton players left them there after a game. When this sculpture was first proposed, one critic objected that the museum's "majestic front lawn does not need to be cluttered with silly pop-art." Public dispute grew bitter over this artwork, but it is now a great tourist attraction and a distinctive landmark.

Another Kansas City landmark, the Kemper Museum of Contemporary Art and Design, contains modern art, like the paintings of Georgia O'Keefe, who made richly colored close-up views of flowers. The Kemper Museum's entrance is guarded by an enormous bronze spider.

Kansas City's museums don't just contain art. The *Arabia* Steam-

Downtown Kansas City's many fountains make it a refreshing place to take a break.

A man relaxing on the lawn of the Nelson-Atkins Museum of Art is dwarfed by the enormous badminton birdie sculpture nearby.

boat Museum is certainly worth a visit. In 1856 the steamboat *Arabia* hit a log snag while going up the Missouri River. It sank, carrying two hundred tons of cargo to the bottom. Flooding later caused the river to change course, and the sunken boat ended up buried in a farmer's field in Kansas. In 1989, it was dug out from under forty-five feet of mud. The museum contains the objects recovered from the sunken boat—the largest collection of pre–Civil War artifacts in existence. Being buried deep in mud helped to preserve much of the cargo, since the lack of oxygen prevented things from rusting and decaying. They even dug out glass bottles of pickles, and the pickles were still bright green and tasty looking!

Another unusual museum in Kansas City is the Toy and Miniature Museum. Housed in a 1911 mansion, this collection boasts antique toys and small-scale replicas of houses, furniture, and objects. Many of the miniature objects are functional—scissors cut, clocks can be wound, and musical instruments can be played. "I'm not interested in dolls," said one Kansas City resident, "but the Miniature Museum was great. I was surprised. Everyone I know who's been there really liked it. Even boys like it."

After all your sightseeing in Kansas City, head over to Arthur Bryant's for a delicious barbecue sandwich. They pile smoked meat onto your plate, served with a pickle and two slices of bread—one white, one brown. The dark-brown tangy sauce is in a squeeze bottle at your table. Squeeze some on your sandwich and enjoy a classic Missouri taste!

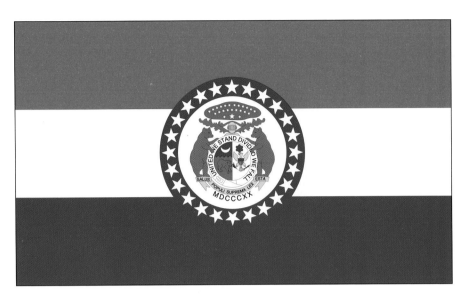

THE FLAG: *Broad red, white, and blue stripes cross Missouri's flag, symbolizing the state's loyalty to the Union. In the flag's center is the state seal surrounded by 24 stars, indicating that Missouri was the 24th state to enter the Union.*

THE SEAL: *In the state seal, two grizzly bears representing Missourians' strength and bravery hold a shield that reads "United We Stand, Divided We Fall." Also on the shield are symbols representing the United States and Missouri.*

STATE SURVEY

Statehood: August 10, 1821

Origin of Name: From the Iliniwek word *Missouri*, which means "owner of big canoes"

Nickname: Show Me State

Capital: Jefferson City

Motto: The welfare of the people shall be the supreme law

Bird: Bluebird

Flower: Hawthorn

Tree: Flowering dogwood

Insect: Honeybee

Mineral: Galena

Rock: Mozarkite

Hawthorn

Bluebird

THE MISSOURI WALTZ

President Harry S. Truman loved to play "The Missouri Waltz" on the piano in the White House. It has been recorded over the years by such performers as Bing Crosby, Guy Lombardo, Gene Autry, and Perry Como. Composed in 1914, it was adopted as the official state song in 1949.

Words by J. R. Shannon　　　　　　　　　**Music by Frederick K. Logan**

Hush - a - bye, my ba - by, slum - ber-time is com - ing soon;

Rest your head up-on my breast while Mom - my hums a tune. The

sand - man is call - ing where shad - ows are fall - ing, While the

soft breez - es sigh as in days long gone by.

'Way down in Mis-sou - ri where I heard this mel - o-dy,

When I was a lit - tle child__ on my Mom - my's knee; The

old folks were hum - ming; Their ban - jos were strum - ming So__

sweet and low.__

GEOGRAPHY

Highest Point: 1,772 feet above sea level, at Taum Sauk Mountain

Lowest Point: 230 feet above sea level, along the St. Francis River near Caldwell

Area: 69,709 square miles

Greatest Distance, North to South: 319 miles

Greatest Distance, East to West: 365 miles

Bordering States: Iowa to the north; Illinois, Kentucky, and Tennessee to the east; Arkansas to the south; Oklahoma, Kansas, and Nebraska to the west

Hottest Recorded Temperature: 118°F at Clinton on July 15, 1936; at Lamar on July 18 1936; and at Union and Warsaw on July 14, 1954

Coldest Recorded Temperature: -40°F at Warsaw on February 13, 1905

Average Annual Precipitation: 40 inches

Major Rivers: Black, Chariton, Current, Gasconade, Grand, Meramec, Mississippi, Missouri, Osage

Major Lakes: Lake of the Ozarks, Pomme de Terre, Stockton, Table Rock, Taneycomo, Harry S. Truman, Mark Twain

Trees: ash, bald cypress, cottonwood, elm, hickory, maple, oak, shortleaf pine, sweet gum

Wild Plants: aster, dogwood, goldenrod, milkweed, mint, mistletoe, rose, verbena, violet

Animals: beaver, cottontail rabbit, fox, muskrat, opossum, raccoon, skunk, squirrel, white-tailed deer

Cottontail rabbit

Birds: Baltimore oriole, blue jay, bobwhite, cardinal, goldfinch, mockingbird, purple finch, whippoorwill, woodpecker

Fish: bass, bluegill, catfish, crappie, jack salmon, trout

Endangered Animals: Curtis pearlymussell, fat pocketbook, gray bat, Higgens eye, Indiana bat, least tern, Ozark big-eared bat, pallid sturgeon, pink mucket, Topeka shiner

Least tern

Endangered Plants: Missouri bladderpod, pondberry, running buffalo clover

TIMELINE

Missouri History

1500s The Osage, Delaware, Shawnee, and other Indians live in what is now Missouri

1673 French explorers Jacques Marquette and Louis Jolliet are likely the first Europeans to see the mouth of the Missouri River

1682 France claims Missouri

1735 The first permanent white settlement in Missouri is established at Ste. Genevieve

1764 St. Louis is founded

1774 The first school in Missouri opens

1803 Missouri becomes U.S. territory as part of the Louisiana Purchase

1804 Meriwether Lewis and William Clark leave St. Louis on their journey to explore the Louisiana Purchase

1808 The *Missouri Gazette*, Missouri's first newspaper, begins publication in St. Louis

1811 The second-worst earthquake in U.S. history strikes New Madrid

1812 Missouri Territory is established

1817 The *Zebulon Pike* becomes the first steamboat to travel up the Mississippi River to St. Louis

1821 Missouri becomes the 24th state

1825 The Osage Indians surrender the last of their lands in Missouri and move west to Kansas

1841 The first wagon trains to travel the Oregon Trail leave Independence

1849 Fire destroys most of downtown St. Louis

1851 Missouri's first railroad is built

1854 Border wars erupt between proslavery Missourians and antislavery Kansans

1857 The U.S. Supreme Court rules that Missourian Dred Scott must remain a slave, even though he has lived in free territories

1860 The first Pony Express riders leave St. Joseph, Missouri, carrying mail bound for California

1861–1865 The Civil War

1873 The nation's first public kindergarten opens in St. Louis

1882 The notorious outlaw Jesse James is killed in St. Joseph

1904 St. Louis hosts a world's fair

1917–1918 More than 140,000 Missourians fight in World War I

1931 The Osage River is dammed, creating Lake of the Ozarks

1941 The United States enters World War II

1945 Missourian Harry Truman becomes president; the state's fourth and present constitution is adopted

1965 The Gateway Arch in St. Louis is completed

1986 Missouri begins operating a lottery

Apple picking

ECONOMY

Agricultural Products: apples, beef cattle, chickens, corn, dairy products, hogs, peaches, sorghum, soybeans, turkeys, wheat

Manufactured Products: airplanes, automobiles, beer, cans, chemicals, food products, printed materials, railroad cars

Natural Resources: clay, coal, iron ore, lead, limestone, sand and gravel

Business and Trade: banking, insurance, real estate, telecommunications, transportation, wholesale and retail trade

CALENDAR OF CELEBRATIONS

Eagle Days Each January bird lovers flock to Clarksville to watch eagles dive and swoop and fish near 500-foot-tall bluffs along the Mississippi. The event also features special eagle exhibits and eagle-viewing tours.

Wurstfest In March the historic German town of Hermann honors that traditional German delicacy, the sausage, with a festival featuring sausage-making demonstrations and lots of tasty samples.

St. Louis Storytelling Festival Some of the best storytellers in the nation captivate listeners at this May event.

Hermann Maifest

Lewis and Clark Rendezvous See how people lived in Missouri's early days at this May event in St. Charles. History buffs bring the lives of fur traders, Indians, and soldiers to life, and craftspeople sell their handmade wares.

Scott Joplin Ragtime Festival Music lovers from all over the world descend on Sedalia each June to listen to lively music, trade sheet music, and learn more about the ragtime master.

Ozark Empire Fair The second-largest fair in Missouri, Springfield's Ozark Empire Fair in late July and early August includes livestock competitions featuring llamas, rabbits, goats, and other animals, a petting zoo, parades, and lots of carnival rides and fun fair food.

Moonlight Ramble The world's largest nighttime bicycle event, this August extravaganza in St. Louis begins in the evening with clinics and demonstrations. But the main event doesn't start until midnight, when the bicyclists head off on a 20-mile tour.

Japanese Festival Each September the Missouri Botanical Garden in St. Louis honors Japanese culture. During the day, you can take in traditional food, music, and crafts, and then at night you can stroll through the lovely Japanese Garden, where lanterns line the paths and light up the water.

Prairie Day Hayrides, music, and crafts demonstrations are all part of this celebration of pioneer life each September in Diamond.

Festival of America Silver Dollar City hosts the nation's largest gathering of craftspeople each September and October. You can see stained glass artisans, dollmakers, and glassblowers demonstrate their art, hear lots of foot-stomping music, and munch on foods from across the nation.

Deutsch Country Days Find out how Missouri's early German immigrants lived at this October event in Marthasville. Sheepshearing, wool dying, rug making, and dozens of other crafts are demonstrated.

Applefest Celebration Press your own apple cider, enjoy delicious apple dumplings or apple butter, and then wash it all down with homemade root beer. Many visitors also buy apples grown in nearby orchards at this October festival in Weston.

Festival of Lights During the holiday season millions of lights blaze brightly in Springfield. Hundreds of displays fill the fairgrounds, and a decorated train zips around town.

STATE STARS

Robert Altman (1925–   ) is a director famous for his innovative, irreverent films, such as *Nashville* and *The Player*, which often have lots of characters and interweaving stories. Early in his career, he directed television programs, including episodes of *Alfred Hitchcock Presents* and

Bonanza. He first gained widespread attention with his 1970 movie *M*A*S*H*, about the antics of a medical unit in the Korean War. This was soon followed by such masterpieces as *McCabe and Mrs. Miller* and *The Long Goodbye*. Altman was born in Kansas City.

Josephine Baker (1906–1975) was a flamboyant dancer and singer born in St. Louis. Her career took her to New York, where she gained fame performing in nightclubs. In 1925 she went to Paris, where she was a sensation. She is credited with introducing Europeans to many African-American dances and styles. Baker decided to remain in Paris and eventually became a French citizen.

Josephine Baker

Yogi Berra (1925–   ), one of baseball's most popular figures and greatest catchers, was born in St. Louis. Berra was an outstanding defensive player. He once went 148 games without a single error. He was also a dangerous hitter, able to power all sorts of pitches out of the park for

home runs. Berra played on ten World Series–winning New York Yankees teams, a record. More than anything, Berra is beloved for his sense of humor and skewed sayings, such as "Baseball is 90 percent mental. The other half is physical." He was elected to the National Baseball Hall of Fame in 1972.

Yogi Berra

Chuck Berry (1926–   ), who grew up in St. Louis, was one of the most important figures in early rock and roll, mixing rhythm and blues and country with rock and roll. His first hit, "Maybelline," in 1955, scored big on the pop, rhythm and blues, and country and western charts. He also wrote such classics as "Roll over Beethoven" and "Johnny B. Goode." Berry was a wild performer, able to dance and play guitar at the same time, a feat perfected in his famous duck walk. His combination of rhythm and blues and rock and roll had a huge influence on later performers such as the Beatles and the Rolling Stones.

Omar Bradley (1893–1981) was a general who commanded the largest group of U.S. troops ever amassed—more than a million soldiers—for the invasion of Europe during World War II. His brilliant leadership and concern for his troops made him tremendously popular. In 1949, President Harry Truman appointed him the first chairman of the Joint Chiefs of Staff. Bradley was born in Clark.

Omar Bradley

William Wells Brown (1815–1884) was the first African American to publish a novel, the first to publish a drama, and the first to publish a travel book. Brown was born a slave in Kentucky and taken to St. Louis as a child. In 1834, he escaped north, where he was educated and became a popular speaker about life in the American South. He published his first book, an autobiography entitled *The Narrative of*

William W. Brown, in 1847. In the next 11 years, he published his other landmark works.

Adolphus Busch (1839–1913), one of the nation's most successful beer makers, was born in Germany. He moved to the United States in 1857 and settled in St. Louis. Busch entered the brewing business of his father-in-law, Eberhard Anheuser, in 1866. Within a few years, Busch began treating the beer so it could withstand changes in temperature and be shipped all over the country. By 1901, Anheuser-Busch was the nation's biggest brewing company. Busch also developed Budweiser, the world's most popular beer.

Walter Cronkite (1916–   ) was one of the country's most trusted journalists. He first made his name as a newspaper correspondent covering World War II in Europe. In 1950, he began working for CBS and helped to develop its television news department. He served as the anchor of the *CBS Evening News* from 1962 to 1981. Cronkite was born in St. Joseph.

Walt Disney (1901–1966) was the world's most famous animator and the creator of the vast Disney empire. He was born in Illinois, but his family moved to Missouri when he was an infant, and he grew up in Marceline and St. Louis. He began doing animation in Kansas City and in 1923 moved to Hollywood. He began producing his own cartoons and soon

Walt Disney

came up with his most famous character, Mickey Mouse. Disney's studio went on to produce such animated classics as *Snow White and the Seven Dwarves* and *Fantasia*, along with such live-action films as *Mary Poppins*. In 1955, Disney opened Disneyland, the first of his theme parks.

T. S. Eliot (1888–1965) was a poet who helped reshape modern literature. Eliot grew up in St. Louis, moved to London, England, in 1914, and eventually became a British citizen. In 1917, his poem "The Love Song of J. Alfred Prufrock" was published. It shook up the poetry world with its use of humor and cliches. But his real triumph was his long, difficult poem *The Waste Land*, about the corruption of contemporary life, which was filled with obscure references, sometimes in other languages. Eliot was awarded the Nobel Prize for literature, the world's greatest literary honor, in 1948.

Betty Grable (1916–1973) was one of the biggest movie stars of the 1940s. Grable was dancing and singing in movie chorus lines by age 14. She soon graduated to starring roles, playing energetic, good-natured characters in such lively musicals as *Moon over Miami* and *Down Argentine Way*. She also appeared in such serious films as *I Wake Up Screaming* and *A Yank in the R.A.F.* Grable was born in St. Louis.

Robert Heinlein (1907–1988), a Butler native, was one of science fiction's greatest writers. An engineer, Heinlein used his scientific background to make his dozens of novels realistic. His books are renowned for their detail and for predicting scientific advancements, such as the development of atomic power. Heinlein won the Hugo Award for the year's best science fiction novel a record four times, for *Stranger in a Strange Land*, *The Moon Is a Harsh Mistress*, *Starship Troopers*, and *Double Star*. He also wrote many science fiction novels for young people, including *Citizen of the Galaxy* and *Time for the Stars*.

Langston Hughes (1902–1967), a writer from Joplin, was a major figure in the Harlem Renaissance, the flowering of arts in New York's most famous African-American community in the 1920s. Hughes made literary history by using the rhythms of jazz and blues in his poems, such as "The Negro Speaks of Rivers." By the end of his life, Hughes had produced more than 50 books, including the poetry collection *Weary Blues*, the novel *Not without Laughter*, and the short story collection *The Ways of White Folks*.

Langston Hughes

Jesse James (1847–1882), an outlaw who became a legend, was born in Clay County. During the Civil War, he was part of a gang of pro-Confederate raiders who wreaked havoc on pro-Union people in Kansas and Missouri. After the war, he and his brother Frank and the Younger brothers formed a gang of bank and train robbers. He was eventually killed by one of his own men, who was trying to collect the reward for his capture.

Marianne Moore (1887–1972), one of America's greatest poets, was born in St. Louis. Moore wrote carefully constructed, difficult poems, often about nature. In 1952, she was awarded the Pulitzer Prize for her book *Collected Poems*. She also edited the *Dial* literary magazine for several years, using the position to encourage young writers.

J. C. Penney (1875–1971), who was from Hamilton, founded the J.C. Penney Company in 1913. By his retirement in 1946, there were more than 1,600 J.C. Penney department stores across the nation. J.C. Penney remains one of the country's largest retailers today.

John J. Pershing (1860–1948) commanded American forces in Europe in World War I. He is renowned for maintaining the spirit of his troops and for using an aggressive, driving style of warfare that contrasted sharply with the trench warfare that European troops had been using. After the war, he was given the rank General of the Armies of the United States, the highest rank ever granted to an American army officer. Pershing was from Laclede.

John J. Pershing

Joseph Pulitzer (1847–1911), a newspaper publisher, was born in Hungary. In 1864, he moved to St. Louis, where he became a reporter and a member of the Missouri House of Representatives. He purchased the *St. Louis Dispatch* and *Evening Post* in 1878 and combined them to make the *St. Louis Post-Dispatch*. He later bought the *New York World*, which became famous for its vigorous reporting and exposés. By 1887, it had the largest circulation of any newspaper in the nation. Pulitzer established the Pulitzer Prizes for excellence in journalism, literature, and music.

Joseph Pulitzer

Ginger Rogers (1911–1995), an actor and dancer, is best remembered for her graceful dancing with Fred Astaire in such classic films as *Top Hat* and *Swing Time*. She also appeared in nonmusicals including *Roxie Hart* and *The Major and the Minor*. Rogers, who often played tough, wisecracking characters, won an Academy Award for Best Actress for *Kitty Foyle*. She was born in Independence.

Casey Stengel (1889–1975), one of the greatest managers in baseball history, was born in Kansas City. After many years as an outfielder, in 1931, Stengel became the manager of the Brooklyn Dodgers. He managed several different teams before settling in with the New York Yankees in 1949. He guided them to a World Series championship his very first year. The Yankees went on to win five World Series in a row and a total of seven with Stengel at the helm. Stengel was elected to the National Baseball Hall of Fame in 1966.

Harry Truman (1884–1972) was the 33rd president of the United States. Truman was known for his forthrightness and his willingness to take responsibility for his decisions, which made him both popular and controversial. Only a few months after becoming president, Truman made the decision to drop two atomic bombs on Japan, which ended World War II. He also oversaw the beginning of the Cold War, the long-standing hostility between the former Soviet Union and the United States. Truman was born in Lamar.

Mark Twain (1835–1910), one of America's favorite writers, was born in Florida, Missouri, and grew up in Hannibal. Twain worked as a printer, steamboat pilot, and miner before settling in as a writer. He first gained attention for his story "The Celebrated Jumping Frog of Calaveras County." His fame endures for such Missouri-set novels as *The Adventures of Tom*

Sawyer and *The Adventures of Huckleberry Finn*. Twain was one of the first writers to portray America with everyday language and humor. This paved the way for later American writers to use less formal language.

Tom Watson (1949–   ) is one of the best golfers ever. After a few shaky years, by 1977 he had established himself as the top player of the time, famed for his putting mastery. Six times he was named the Professional Golfers' Association Player of the Year. Watson was born in Kansas City.

Tom Watson

Tennessee Williams (1911–1983), a leading playwright, wrote dramas with a strong southern atmosphere. Williams's plays are highly emotional and poetic and often focus on rather odd characters. Some people consider *A Streetcar Named Desire*, which earned Williams the 1948 Pulitzer Prize for drama, the best American play ever. He won the Pulitzer again six years later for *Cat on a Hot Tin Roof*. Both were turned into successful films. Williams grew up in St. Louis.

Shelley Winters (1922–   ) is an actress who began her career playing sultry roles but became more famous for her blowzy, loudmouthed characters. Winters earned Best Supporting Actress Oscars for her performances in *The Diary of Anne Frank* and *A Patch of Blue*. Some of her other famous films include *Lolita* and *The Night of the Hunter*. She is from St. Louis.

TOUR THE STATE

Gateway Arch (St. Louis) This gleaming 630-foot monument honors St. Louis's 19th-century role as the Gateway to the West.

City Museum (St. Louis) Walk through the mouth of a giant whale, find the hidden staircase in an old fort, or get lost in the manmade caves at this magical museum.

St. Louis Science Center Feel the earth move in a simulated earthquake, hear a huge dinosaur roar, and climb into a cave at this museum filled with hundreds of interactive exhibits.

Missouri Botanical Garden (St. Louis) After gazing at lots of exotic, flowering plants and making your way through a hedge maze, you may want to take a breather in the peaceful Japanese Garden.

Museum of Transportation (St. Louis) This museum has one of the biggest collections of railroad cars in the country, along with a huge number of cars, trucks, and buses. There's even a tugboat you can explore.

St. Louis Iron Mountain and Southern Railway (Jackson) Climb aboard an old-time railroad car and then listen to the steam engine pull you along the tracks in a trip back in time.

Johnson's Shut-Ins State Park (Piedmont) Slip and slide down natural waterslides in this park full of stunning gorges and dramatic boulders.

Elephant Rocks State Park (Graniteville) A line of

St. Louis Iron Mountain and Southern Railway

huge rocks gives this park its name. After exploring the boulders, you might want to try your hand at fishing.

Onondaga Cave (Leasburg) You'll see extraordinary formations and learn all about the creatures that live underground on a visit to this cave.

Ozark National Scenic Riverways (Van Buren) People come from all over to canoe or raft down the Current and Jack's Fork Rivers through dense forests and past looming bluffs.

Laura Ingalls Wilder and Rose Wilder Lane Home and Museum (Mansfield) On a visit to the house where the author of the Little House series spent most of her life, you'll find lots of family pictures and possessions along with displays about pioneer times.

Glade Top Trail (Ava) The views are spectacular on this scenic byway, especially when the wildflowers are in bloom or when the leaves explode in a riot of color. It's also a great place to spy wildlife such as wild turkeys and roadrunners.

Ha Ha Tonka State Park (Camdenton) The ruins of a magnificent castle overlooking the Lake of the Ozarks are the centerpiece of this park. Visitors can also traipse along trails that pass by natural bridges, through collapsed caves, and near bubbling streams.

Hank Weinmeister's House of Butterflies (Osage Beach) Hundreds of butterflies fly among the lush plants here, sometimes landing on flowers and sometimes on visitors' heads.

State Capitol (Jefferson City) Don't miss the Thomas Hart Benton mural on the tour of this magnificent domed building.

American Jazz Museum (Kansas City) At this museum, you can learn all about jazz and some of its greatest performers, including Kansas Citian Charlie Parker. You can also experiment with recording equipment in a studio and sometimes even hear live performances.

Pony Express National Memorial (St. Joseph) The stables where the Pony Express riders took off with their mailbags bound for California are now a museum. Exhibits let visitors choose the best horse for the ride, send a telegraph message, and experience some of the sights and sounds of the long trip.

Squaw Creek National Wildlife Refuge (Mound City) Pelicans, eagles, and snow geese are just a few of the birds you might see during a visit to this marshy spot.

FUN FACTS

Missouri has more than 5,500 caves, more than any other state.

The first parachute jump ever took place outside St. Louis on March 1, 1912. Captain Albert Berry leapt from a plane flying at 1,500 feet.

The 1904 world's fair in St. Louis produced lots of tasty firsts. The world's first ice cream cone was served there, along with the first cotton candy, the first hot dog on a bun, and the first iced tea.

FIND OUT MORE

Do you want to learn more about Missouri? You might start by checking your local bookstore or library or the Internet for these titles.

GENERAL STATE BOOKS

Fradin, Dennis Brindell. *Missouri*. Chicago, IL: Children's Press, 1995.

Thompson, Kathleen. *Missouri*. Austin, TX: Raintree/Steck-Vaughn, 1996.

SPECIAL INTEREST BOOKS

Beveridge, Thomas R., and Jerry D. Vineyard. *Geologic Wonders and Curiosities of Missouri*. Rolla, MO: Missouri Department of Natural Resources, 1990.

Hiscock, Bruce. *The Big Rivers: The Missouri, the Mississippi, and the Ohio*. New York: Atheneum, 1997.

Lourie, Peter. *In the Path of Lewis and Clark: Traveling the Missouri*. Parsippany, NJ: Silver Burdett, 1997.

Tedrow, Thomas L. *The Legend of the Missouri Mud Monster*. Nashville, TN: Thomas Nelson, 1996.

Wilder, Laura Ingalls. *On the Way Home*. New York: HarperCollins, 1994.

FICTION

Clements, Bruce. *I Tell a Lie Every So Often*. New York: Farrar, Straus & Giroux, 1984. In 1848, a 14-year-old boy tells two lies with the result that he and his brother must travel up the Missouri River to look for a missing cousin.

Twain, Mark. *The Adventures of Tom Sawyer*. 1876. New York: Dover, 1998. Tom and his best friend Huck go treasure hunting in the caves by the river and witness a terrible crime.

VIDEOS

Jesse James. Twentieth Century Fox, 1939. This dramatic western shows Jesse's career of bank and train robbery, and his tragic end. Filmed in Missouri.

Meet Me in St. Louis. Metro Goldwyn Meyer, 1944. A light-hearted musical about a family in St. Louis at the time of the 1904 world's fair, starring Judy Garland.

The Sting. Universal Studios, 1973. An action-packed tale of 1930s con men conning each other. The soundtrack is pure Scott Joplin.

WEBSITES

Missouri State Home Page. www.state.mo.us

Missouri's Department of Natural Resources (a great guide to state parks and historic sites). www.dnr.state.mo.us

Missouri Tourism. www.missouritourism.org

INDEX

Page numbers for charts, graphs, and illustrations are in boldface.